The Way, The Truth and The Life

Pupil's Book 6

Author

Sr. Marcellina Cooney CP

Co-ordinating Editor

Angela Edwards

Editorial Team

Rufina Ebenebe, Brendan Flavin, Louise Kenny-Hodgson,
Rudolf Loewenstein OP, Rose Murphy, Carmela Puccio, Pippa Smart

Teachers' Enterprise in Religious Education Co. Ltd

Introduction

Welcome to *The Way, the Truth and the Life* series.

Jesus said: "I am the Way, the Truth and the Life" (Jn 14:6)
These are very important words, so I would like each one of you to
ask Jesus to help you to understand them.

In your lessons in Religious Education this year, you will explore
the important questions young people ask in order to deepen their
understanding of **who** Jesus is, **what** they believe about him and
his Church and **why** they believe it.

You will learn about the Kingdom of God and His love, mercy and justice for all people.
In Exploring the Mass, you will have the opportunity to reflect on how to participate
more fully in the Eucharist, and how it helps us in our daily lives.

The module on Jesus the Messiah begins with big questions from young people and
explores in great depth the passion, death, resurrection and ascension of Jesus and what
it means for us. This leads on to the transforming power of the Spirit of Jesus on the
Apostles, in particular Saints Peter and Paul. You will also learn about some of the recent
successors of St. Peter.

The last section of the book focuses on the Sacraments of Confirmation, Matrimony and
Holy Orders. It highlights some inspirational people and the very important task that
young people are called to in the Church today.

I hope you will enjoy your study this year and that each day you will grow closer to Jesus,
who loves us and sends us his peace.

Vincent Nichols

✠ His Eminence Cardinal Vincent Nichols
   Archbishop of Westminster

Contents

1. The Kingdom of God

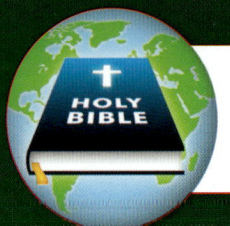

Know about the Kingdom of God.
Reflect on its meaning for us.

What? Why? Where?

Many people are puzzled about the Kingdom of God. Here are some of the questions pupils have asked. As these questions are very important, they will be answered over the following weeks.

What is the Kingdom of God like? Will everyone be happy all the time?   Chris

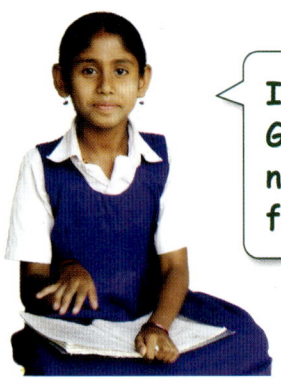

Is the Kingdom of God in heaven? If not, where can I find it? Sabrina

Is the Kingdom of God for everyone?

What about people who do not believe in God?   Enzo

What do we have to do in order to be in the Kingdom?   Jane

Expectations …!   When Jesus came to earth, people had been expecting the arrival of the Messiah as a great and powerful warrior or king, one who would conquer their enemies. They were expecting an extraordinary event.

"Being asked by the Pharisees when the Kingdom of God was coming, Jesus answered them, 'The Kingdom of God is not coming with signs to be observed; nor will they say, 'Here it is or there it is!' **For behold, the Kingdom of God is in the midst of you'"** (Lk 17:20-21).

Values of the Kingdom of God

LOVE: to choose to be compassionate, helpful and kind

FORGIVENESS: accept an apology and make an apology

PEACE: good will and harmony

FREEDOM: to choose to do what is right

TRUTH: to have the courage to say what is true

FAITH: belief and confidence in God

HOPE: to trust in God especially when it is hard to do so

JUSTICE: to be fair and honest with others

COURAGE: to stand up for what is right

GOODNESS: to be generous in helping others

Activities

1. Working in groups, choose the value you think is the most important and share reasons to justify your opinions.

2. Choose three values. Give examples of how each one you have chosen could be put into practice:
   - at home,
   - in school.

What is the Kingdom of God like?

Jesus explained that the Kingdom of God is here now. It starts within us and spreads. It is when we are **merciful**, **thoughtful** and **compassionate** to one another that the Kingdom of God grows and spreads throughout the world. Jesus gives the example of a woman making bread.

Parable of the Yeast

"It is like the yeast a woman took and mixed in with three measures of flour till it was leavened all through" (Lk 13:20-21).

This parable suggests that the Kingdom of God is like something that starts small and grows quietly and powerfully until it changes things completely.

Pause to reflect

Share with the person next to you. How do kind words and thoughtful actions make you feel? Imagine what it would be like if everybody made a special effort every day to be kind to others.

Parable of the mustard seed

"The Kingdom of God is like a grain of mustard seed, which, when sown upon the ground, is the smallest of all seeds on earth; yet once it is sown it grows up and becomes the greatest of all shrubs, and puts out large branches, so that the birds of the air can make nests in its shade" (Mk 4:30-32).

The little things we do to help others: for example, a kind word, a helpful hand, being willing to share whatever we have, are indications that God is able to work through us and spread peace and happiness among people.

 Pope Francis explains that the Kingdom of God is hidden within us like a seed in the ground: but it becomes great by the power of the Holy Spirit. We need to let it grow in us, without boasting about it. "Let the Spirit come, change our soul and carry us forward in silence, in peace, in prayer, worship and kind deeds."

He says that the efforts we make to do good things are part of the Kingdom of God.

Examples: it may be that you notice a pupil who is upset or lonely and you make a special effort to be his or her friend. Someone is in trouble or unable to do their work and you offer to help.

 Each day there are opportunities in school or at home to be thoughtful and compassionate to others. These are the seeds of kindness which are planted. We may never know how much we have helped others but, we trust that God is working in and through us. Every effort we make to be helpful will bring about a rich harvest of good deeds.

Activity

Write replies to the questions by Sabrina and Chris.

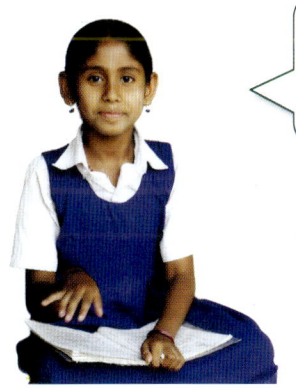

Is the Kingdom of God in heaven? If not, where can I find it?
Sabrina

What is the Kingdom of God like?
Chris

The Kingdom is for All

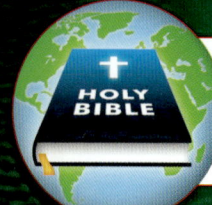

Understand that everyone is invited into the Kingdom of God. Consider ways to share this Good News.

Jesus cares about everyone

Jesus wants all people to belong to his Kingdom. He wants people of every race, culture, age, ability, the good, the bad and the simply not interested.

The **Good News** that Jesus brought for all people is that the Kingdom of God is for everyone. It is for the poor, the lonely, the sick, the unemployed, the refugees, the prisoners and all people of good will.

God wants even those who have not heard of the Kingdom to be part of it. Those who have drifted away from God still belong to Him. There is great joy in heaven when they return to Him. If there is even one person missing, Jesus will search to find him or her.

Jesus told the parable of the lost sheep to explain that no matter how many people are already safe in the Kingdom, he will always search out those who have gone astray to bring them back to God. Jesus explains what God is like in the parable of the 'lost sheep'.

Parable of the Lost Sheep

"Which man among you, having a hundred sheep and losing one of them, does not leave the ninety-nine in the wilderness and go after the one which is lost, until he finds it?

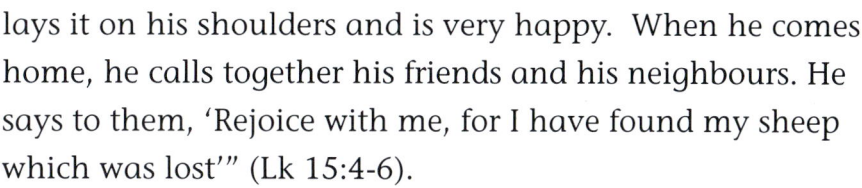

When he has found the lost sheep, he lays it on his shoulders and is very happy. When he comes home, he calls together his friends and his neighbours. He says to them, 'Rejoice with me, for I have found my sheep which was lost'" (Lk 15:4-6).

Parable of the Lost Drachma

Jesus invites those listening to him to consider, "What woman with ten drachma (silver coins) would not, if she lost one, light a lamp and sweep out the house and

search thoroughly till she found it? And then, when she had found it, call together her friends and neighbours, 'Rejoice with me,' she would say, 'I have found the drachma I lost'. In the same way, I tell you, there is rejoicing among the angels of God over one repentant sinner" (Lk 15:8-10).

No matter what we have done or how sinful we may imagine ourselves to be, or how far away we feel from God, God loves us personally, He will never give up on us. St Catherine of Siena said, "Don't you understand? God is running after you day and night as though He has nothing to do but simply to occupy Himself with you".

The Prodigal Son

Use the Bible. Read the Parable of the Prodigal Son (Lk 15:11-32).

In this parable, the son, by demanding his share of the inheritance, is treating his father as if he were already dead. The father did not want him to leave home and drift away from the family. However, the father respected his freedom to choose and did not force him to stay.

Eventually, when the son had spent his inheritance, ruined his life and lost his so-called friends, he reflected on what he had done. He decided to go home and seek forgiveness. His father who was looking out for him, rushed to welcome him with open arms. He was overcome with joy because his son had returned.

In this parable, we learn that no matter how we have messed up our lives, God always forgives us if we turn to him and seek forgiveness. At every moment, God offers us a future full of hope. For God, it is never 'too late'.

Activities

1. Imagine you have a friend who no longer goes to church and finds it difficult to trust in Jesus.
   Think about what you have been studying. Write out a detailed plan of what you could do to help him or her.

2. Write a modern day parable of a prodigal son or daughter.
   Remember to include repentance and forgiveness.

3. **'THE KINGDOM IS FOR EVERYONE'**
   This is the title of a web page.
   a) Show what the rest of the page will look like.
   b) Remember to include the following: images, text and scripture references.
   c) Provide evidence for your beliefs.

4. People are homeless usually because of misfortune, wrong-choices or both. Frequently they feel lonely, downhearted or even rejected by others.
   Write a letter to explain that the Kingdom of God is for them.
   Give examples from the parables of Jesus.

Commitment to the Kingdom

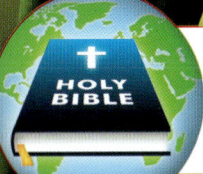

Understand the words and actions necessary to show our commitment to the Kingdom.
Reflect on how we live up to this commitment.

What are the rules?

Rules...

When you go to a new school, the rules and expectations are made very clear and there are sanctions if you don't obey them. So when Jesus shared the Good News of the Kingdom of God with the people, they wanted to know what they would have to do to join it.   Rather than emphasising rules and punishments, Jesus called his followers to a path of love and mercy.

"I give you a New Commandment:
love one another;
just as I have loved you,
you must also love one another"
(Jn 13:34).

Jesus gives an example of how we should love one another in the parable about the Good Samaritan.

The Good Samaritan
Use the Bible. Read Luke 10:29-37.

The people listening to Jesus could not have been more surprised. Jews did not like Samaritans; in fact, they were enemies. This parable turned everything upside down for them.

The priest and the Levite pass a man on the ground, covered with blood and half dead. When a **Samaritan** comes along, he immediately feels compassion and goes over to help him. Before bandaging his wounds, the Samaritan disinfects them with wine and puts oil on to keep them soft. Then he helps the man up onto his own donkey and takes him to an inn. He pays for him to be looked after. On his way back, he calls to see if there are any further expenses owing.

Pause to discuss

Who do you think is our neighbour?
What do you think is the most important message in this parable?
What is the 'Kingdom value' that is required?

INVITATION TO
THE KINGDOM OF GOD

Thinking about it!

In accepting an invitation to the Kingdom of God, we accept to live by its values.

Activities

1. Complete the sentences

    a. When I am FURIOUS, Jesus wants me to …
    b. When I am ANNOYED with others, Jesus wants me to …
    c. When I see others in NEED, Jesus wants me to …
    d. When I prefer to go MY OWN WAY, Jesus wants me to …
    e. When I aim to have LOTS OF THINGS, Jesus wants me to …
    f. When I am ANGRY, Jesus wants me to …
    g. When I aim to GET EVEN, Jesus wants me to …

2. What do you think are the pros and cons of accepting the invitation to belong to the Kingdom of God?

Importance of the New Commandment

When we help our neighbour, especially if that person is someone we don't like, we are living the New Commandment and building up the Kingdom of God on earth. Jesus will remember these good actions and one day, he will say to us,

"Come, O blessed of my Father, inherit the Kingdom prepared
for you from the foundation of the world; for
I was hungry and you gave me food,
I was thirsty and you gave me drink,
I was a stranger and you welcomed me,
I was naked and you clothed me,
I was sick and you visited me,
I was in prison and you came to see me" (Matt 25:34-37).

HELPING - others with food, clothing, something to drink, shelter from very cold weather - deeds which can be summed up as mercy, kindness, thoughtfulness, generosity.

ACTIONS - like giving, welcoming, visiting, taking care of others – deeds which can be summed up as mercy and compassion.

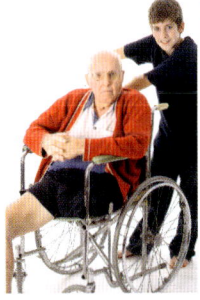   

Activity

a) Work in pairs. List all the opportunities there are to help others:
  - at home,
  - in school,
  - in your local area.

b) Choose two. Explain what you will do to live them out for a week.

c) At the end of the week, describe the impact it had on you and the effect it had on those you helped. *(Make sure to keep a diary).*

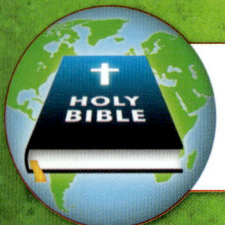

Understand the variety of responses to the Kingdom.
Reflect on our response.

Living life to the full

The Good News of the Kingdom, Jesus tells us, is that he has come to help us to live full and happy lives.

> **"I have come
> so that you may have life
> and have it to the full.
> I am the Good Shepherd:
> the Good Shepherd is the one who lays down his life for his sheep"**
> (Jn 10:10-11).

Jesus promises us life to the full. In order to experience this, he has asked us **to love one another as he has loved us.** Loving God and finding ways to be kind and thoughtful to others is the **KEY** to happiness and living a full life.

Happiness forever

> Will everyone be happy all the time in the Kingdom of God?

It may be that when everyone is fully committed to the Kingdom of God, that there will be peace and happiness in the world. However, not everyone accepts the invitation or knows about it.

When Jesus was on earth, there was suffering and injustice in the world. He was aware of places where people lived in extreme poverty. Some very rich people ignored the suffering of the poor and exploited them. To help people to reflect on situations like this, Jesus told the parable of the rich man and Lazarus.

The rich man and Lazarus

Use the Bible. Read Luke 16:19-31.

In this parable, Jesus is talking about a very powerful, rich man dressed in fine linen. He has a luxurious life, feasting sumptuously every day. Lying at the gate of his mansion is Lazarus, a beggar, covered with sores. This beggar does not even get the crusts that fall from the rich man's table. Stray dogs lick his sores.

Jesus is here describing the terrible injustice in the world: the rich banqueting in palaces and the poor dying of hunger. Suddenly, everything changes. Lazarus dies and is carried off by the angels to heaven. The rich man also dies and goes to Hades, where he is tormented.

When Jesus told this parable to the people, riches were considered a blessing and poverty a curse. Now, Jesus is showing that wealth, accumulated by exploiting the poor, is a terrible injustice which God will bring to an end.

Pause to discuss

What is the most important message in this parable?
Who is likely to draw comfort from it?
Who may want to reject it?
What might be the risks for those who reject it?
What are the rewards for those who listen and act on it?

Activity

Write a report for the school newsletter to explain how your religious beliefs and the teaching of Jesus have influenced your moral values and behaviour. Think about how you live:
- the New Commandment,
- the values of the Kingdom. (Clue p.5)

Invitation to a Banquet (Lk 14:16-24)

Jesus wants us to know that the Kingdom of God is open to all, but not everyone realises the importance of this invitation. To explain what he means, Jesus tells the parable of a man who had a great banquet.

Invited guests who make excuses

Use the Bible. Read Luke 14:16-24.

Pause to discuss and reflect

- Do you think the excuses of the invited guests are genuine? Could any of their activities have been postponed?

- Why do you think the servant was sent to invite the crippled, blind and lame?

- The servant is sent to the open roads and the hedges where the people are likely to be refugees or the homeless. Why do you think he is instructed to force them to come to the banquet?

- Do you think these people would have expected to be invited to a banquet? What might they have thought was going to happen?

- What do you think is the message that Jesus wants the people and us to understand?

- What might be the invitations that Jesus offers us? Do we always accept them? Why or why not?

- Might there be times when we make excuses? Can you give examples?

What about young people today?

> **What can we do for the Kingdom of God?**

Today, it is the responsibility of young people to spread the Good News of the Kingdom of God by words and actions.

To help you do this, Jesus gives through the sacraments:

- strength,
- courage,
- grace to live fully in the Kingdom of God.

Jesus reminds us, "You are the light of the world. A city built on a hill-top cannot be hidden. No one lights a lamp to put it under a bushel; they put it on a lamp-stand where it shines for everyone in the house.

In the same way, you must let your light shine in the sight of people, so that, seeing your good works, they may give glory to your Father who is in heaven" (Matt 5:14-16).

Pause to discuss

In what ways can you be a light to others?
What are some of the good things you do that may inspire others?
In what ways do your good works give glory to God?

Activity

Imagine a friend of yours from abroad comes to visit. She tells you that the government in her country is thinking about closing down Catholic schools.

She wants to write to her prime minister about this and asks you what she can say in support of Catholic schools.

- What advice would you give to her?
- Think deeply before you write down your suggestions.
- Refer to the teaching of Jesus and the values of the Kingdom.

HELPFUL TIPS

The Compassion of Jesus

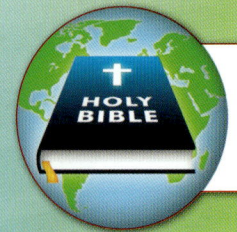

Know that Jesus has compassion on all who suffer.
Think of ways in which we can show compassion.

Mercy and Compassion

The love of Jesus has no boundaries. When he was on earth, Jesus went through all the towns and villages teaching in the synagogues, preaching the Good News of the Kingdom and healing the sick. It did not make any difference if people were rich or poor, saint or sinner, Jesus showed mercy and compassion to everyone who came to him in need.

Jesus did stress the importance of having faith.
To Bartimaeus, the blind man, calling out to him, he said, "What do you want me to do for you?"
The blind man replied, "Master, let me see". Jesus said to him, "Go your way; your faith has made you well" (Mk 10:51-52).

When Jesus saw people by the roadside pleading for pity, he had compassion on them. Jesus made the paralysed man walk again; he healed lepers, restored hearing to the deaf and speech to the dumb. He raised the dead to life and fed thousands who were hungry.

Jesus cured disease as a sign of mercy and compassion for those who were suffering and had faith in him. He was renewing the faith of these people and their trust in God.

Jesus taught the people by his LIFE.
His example showed them that the values of mercy and compassion bring about the Kingdom of God on earth.

Imagine you are a journalist present when one of these miracles takes place. You have to be ready to give a radio or TV report.

Choose one of the miracles in the boxes below. Write your report.

a) Describe what happened.

b) What does it tell us about Jesus?

c) Comment on the effect it had on the person(s).

Scripture references

Cure of a paralytic Mk 2:1-12	**Cure of the blind man** Mk 10:46-52	**Cure of a leper** Mk 1:40-45	**Cure of Simon's mother in law** Mk 1:29-31
Cure of the man with the withered hand Mk 3:1-6	**Five loaves** Mk 6:30-44	**Healing of the deaf man** Mk 7:31-37	**Cure of the Centurion's servant** Lk 7:1-10

d) Work in small groups to practise giving your report within a 60 second time slot.

e) As a class, select about five to be presented at a school assembly.

What is OUR mission?

Our mission is to do all we can to bring signs of God's mercy, compassion and justice into the world. **This is the mission Jesus has entrusted to us.** If we have faith in him, we will witness how he can help us to help others.

Using our Gifts

We are all unique. Each one of us has received special gifts from God. We are now going to think of ways we can use these gifts to share the Good News of the Kingdom of God.

1. Work in groups.

   a) Identify the skills and gifts of each member.

   b) Plan how you can use your skills and gifts to make the Kingdom grow.

   c) Put your plan into action. Share the Good News of the Kingdom, for example, write an article for the school newsletter or write to a newspaper or make a YouTube video for the school website.

ACT NOW

2. Imagine you are to be interviewed on TV or radio.

   a) Write answers to these questions which you are likely to be asked.

   • Where is the Kingdom of God?

   • Who is it for?

   • How do you know everyone is welcome?

   • What do we have to do to be in it?

   • Are there rules?

   • Will we always be happy in it?

   • How can we contribute to it?

   b) Role-play the interview.

BREAKING NEWS

Sharing the Mission

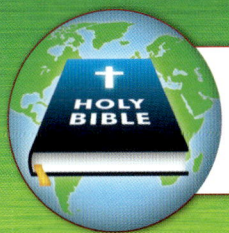

Know about people who helped to spread the Kingdom of God.
Reflect on what we can learn from them.

Mission of the Kingdom

Through the wonders and signs that Jesus worked, he showed us that the Kingdom of God had come. He used parables like the Good Samaritan and the Prodigal Son to help us understand how to live a good life. He performed miracles to show God's mercy and compassion for those who were suffering.

As followers of Jesus, we must be active in showing how much we love God and our neighbour by caring, helping and forgiving others. As St. Teresa of Calcutta used to say, "I don't do great things, but little things with great love".

St. Thérèse of Lisieux (1873 – 1897)

Thérèse Martin was a young French girl with incredible determination. As a child, she decided to be a Carmelite nun. The Mother Superior at the convent in Lisieux told Thérèse she was too young to become a nun. However, Thérèse felt passionately that this was what God wanted for her. She went to Rome to ask the pope if he could give permission. Pope Leo XIII blessed her and told her that she would enter the convent if it was God's will. Soon after that she received permission to enter the convent.

Thérèse wanted to devote her life to helping people. She felt a powerful vocation to help people realise God's tremendous love for them. She said, "I would like to perform the most heroic deeds". However, Thérèse had a terrible temper and had to learn to curb it!

Challenges

Life in the convent had its challenges. The nuns were not all saints and, at times, some of them were difficult. Thérèse recalled how one day, when she and a group of nuns were washing clothes one of them splashed the hot, dirty water into her face, not just once or twice but continually! She felt like throwing a real tantrum, but asked Jesus to help her. She managed to say nothing!

Another nun, Sister St. Pierre, was old and cranky as she struggled to do everything. Thérèse tried to help her to walk along the corridors. "You move too fast," she complained. So Thérèse walked slowly, "Come on, I can't feel your hand, I am going to fall," the old nun grumbled. Thérèse continued to do her best to help her and just smiled. She was offering all these little irritations to Jesus for the spread of the Kingdom.

Even praying in the chapel was not always easy for Thérèse. Each day, there were two hours of prayer and four hours of liturgy. One of the nuns made strange noises as if her dentures were not fitting properly. These sounds really irritated Thérèse. She was almost ready to scream but, instead offered it as a prayer to Jesus. There were other times when she fell asleep at prayer. She was embarrassed about this, but then, she recalled that parents love their children when they are asleep or awake, so she believed God loved her as well.

Thérèse's Mission

Thérèse believed that her mission for the Kingdom consisted in checking her self-will, keeping back an impatient word and doing little things for those around her without their knowing it.

"After my death," she said, "I will spend my heaven in doing good upon earth. I will not be able to take any rest until the end of the world as long as there are souls to be saved." Her advice to us, is to offer to Jesus all the little sacrifices we make.

Thérèse had discovered that LOVE is a dynamic force. It can transform our lives and the life of the world. This happens when we stay close to Jesus, and allow him to work in and through us so that we can love others. Thérèse was able to do this even though her world was an enclosed convent and her only contact was with the nuns.

Thérèse was beatified in 1923 and canonized in 1925. Her feast day is 1 October.

In 2009, when the relics of St. Thérèse of Lisieux toured Great Britain, over 200,000 people went to see them.

Watch the Power Point presentation or research the Internet for details.

a) Why do you think so many people came to see her relics?

b) In what ways do you think you and others are likely to be influenced by her today?

c) How might the example of Thérèse's life give meaning and purpose to the lives of other people?

2. Justice

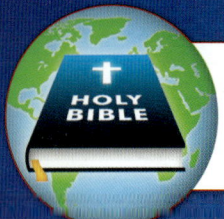

Understand the meaning of justice.
Be aware that we are all called to work for justice.

What is justice?

- Justice involves telling the truth.
- It means being fair to others whether they are friends or enemies.

All justice comes from God. God is just, fair and merciful. He knows that no-one in the world is perfectly good but, He can also see inside our hearts and He understands completely all the reasons why we fail to be good. His love and mercy towards us have no end. This is why He sent Jesus to save us. In return, God asks us to work for justice and mercy in our own time and in the place where we are.

IT'S NOT FAIR ...

Think of the number of times you have heard someone say, 'It's just not fair!' Sometimes we think that injustice happens just in countries at war or where people are starving. It is easy not to notice that injustice can happen at home, at school or in the area where we live. Here are some examples:

It was Friday afternoon. We were all looking forward to games when Mr. Kelly arrived looking very annoyed, "Who broke the window on the corridor?"

Each one of us looked around in search of the guilty person – but no one owned up. So games were cancelled for all of us.

Class 6

I could see how tired Mum was feeling. Like us, she had been at work all day, but she did not complain when we wanted to watch our favourite TV programme. She was left to wash up after dinner – I felt guilty – this was happening too often.

Nada

All through the maths lesson Fred and John took it in turns either to chat or knock their pens on the desk – they could see that Miss Lee was getting very annoyed. She told them to stop it several times, but they kept at it – we were all suffering because Miss Lee was cross.

Jonathan

There are times when we have to stop and think of how our actions will affect others. It takes courage to be fair to other people and to put their needs before our own.

Pause to discuss

Class 6: Was Mr. Kelly right to cancel games for Class 6? Why?
What would you have done?

Nada: Do you think Nada was right to feel guilty? Why?
What advice would you want to give to Nada?

Jonathan: In what ways were Fred and John being unjust to:

- the class?
- the teacher?
- themselves?

Look again at the three examples. In each one:

- what were the injustices?
- what were the possible consequences ?

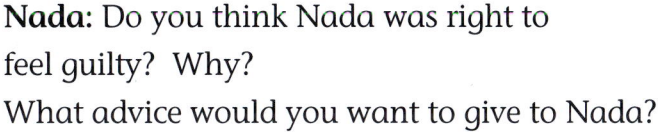

Justice means that...

"Everyone has the right to a standard of living which is adequate for the health and well-being of him/herself and family, including food, clothing, housing, medical care and necessary social services.... Everyone has the right to education." *Universal Declaration of Human Rights*

This declaration comes from the United Nations which is one of the many organisations promoting justice. In spite of this declaration, many people still experience great injustice because of war, poverty, famine or violence.

The Price of Gold

In 2000, when a large mining company came to Honduras in Central America, the people looked forward to new jobs in the gold mine and a better standard of living. They did not realise the changes that were coming.

The Local People

The local people were moved away from their land so that machines could begin excavating the huge mine. They were given new homes but, not enough land to grow crops to sell at market. Soon the walls of their homes began cracking because of explosions from the mine.

The Honduran Government had given the company permission to use 800 litres of water a minute. This meant that the water sources used by local people ran dry. They had to buy water or use water from a tank supplied by the company, but that water wasn't safe to drink. The chemicals used in gold production had got into the water. "We know we are drinking poison," said an old man. Many people developed health problems. They complained about pains in their arms and legs, trouble with eyesight and breathing difficulties. One little girl was born with very soft bones and could not sit up or stand. The local people were sure these problems were linked to the polluted water. Two independent studies found dangerous levels of arsenic and lead in the blood of the local people.

Truth is revealed

News of the situation became known outside the area. Secret films were made and posted on YouTube and campaigns protesting about the conditions took place in several countries.

In 2007, the company announced they were closing the mine. The local community met with the management and asked that five conditions should be met before the company left. The company agreed to their demands. Today, chickens, pigs and cattle are farmed on the former mine site. There is a training centre for the local community. The mine buildings have been remodelled as a hotel for eco-tourism. It creates jobs for local people and attracts new investment to the area.

Activities

1. We are all stewards of God's creation.
   In what ways did the Gold Mining Company:
   a) abuse its stewardship?
   b) misuse its authority?

2. Imagine you are a villager who will be meeting the mine manager to discuss the mine closure. Write a list of five things you feel the company should do to help the people and restore the area before it leaves. You need to give good reasons for each item on your list.

Refugees

A refugee is a person who is outside their home country because they have suffered (or feared) persecution on account of race, religion, nationality or political opinions.

Many refugees have to move in order to save their lives. They have no protection from their own government. In fact, it is often their own government that is threatening to persecute them. If other countries do not let them in, then they may be condemning them to death or to an intolerable life living in extreme poverty and without the right to work.

Some refugees are called migrants. These are the people who choose to move from their own country in order to improve the future prospects for themselves and their families. Many of them are on the verge of starvation; they have no means of earning a living.

The following poem describes the injustice faced by those who have to leave their homes.

Refugees

Secretly, we moved forward,
drawn by dreams of a better life
leaving our homes
where nothing grows.

It was fear that urged us on,
fear of hunger and starvation.
We were stripped at gunpoint as
we neared the frontier.

We carried nothing with us
but memories of love that bound us together.

Activities

1. Analyse the poem 'Refugees'. List the sufferings, hopes and fears in it.

Suffering	Hopes	Fears

2. The government wants to restrict the number of refugees coming into the country.
   Prepare for a debate on this issue.
   Identify reasons for and against restricting numbers.
   (You should think about the teaching of Jesus and the declaration of human rights).

Know about some people who have been persecuted for speaking out about injustice.
Reflect on the cost of commitment.

Oscar Romero (1917-1980)

Oscar Romero lived in El Salvador in Central America. He was ordained a priest in 1942 and became the Archbishop in 1977.

- He was aware that the wealth of the country was in the hands of a small number of families.
- He saw that the vast majority of people lived in great poverty.
- He knew that the poor lived in hovels made of cardboard and corrugated sheeting, without running water or electricity.

In 1979, the Revolutionary Government Junta gained power. They were ruthless in their treatment of the poor. Basic human rights were ignored as the army carried out a brutal regime against the civilian population. Hundreds of people

disappeared, were beaten, imprisoned without trial or killed. Priests and nuns were tortured and murdered for showing sympathy for the poor. Archbishop Romero spoke out on behalf of the people. Even though public meetings were forbidden, he encouraged public demonstrations. He demanded explanations from the government about the murder of certain priests. He called on Church leaders to become the voice of the poor. He said:

"The world that the Church must serve is the world of the poor. Persecution of the Church is the result of defending the poor".

It was very clear to all that the Archbishop was on the side of the poor and those suffering injustice. He even opened his own official residence to the refugees and those hunted for doing good. He allowed a radio station to be set up in the office of the cathedral. It broadcast reports of the unjust actions of the government and the powerful wealthy class.

Each Sunday, huge crowds gathered for the Mass celebrated by the Archbishop and his sermon was broadcast on the radio. The government and the military were extremely worried. This Archbishop was preaching about the rights of the poor.

Archbishop Romero had known for some time that his life was in danger. About two months before his death he wrote in a Mexican newspaper:

"My life has been threatened many times. I have to confess that, as a Christian, I don't believe in death without resurrection...

As a shepherd, I am obliged to give my life for those I love, for the entire Salvadorian people, including those who threaten to assassinate me."

Archbishop Romero was murdered in March 1980 as he was celebrating Mass. At the consecration, a shot rang out and he was killed instantly. The spirit of Oscar Romero lives on today in the Salvadorian people: they continue to struggle against injustice and oppression as he did. His courage and determination continue to be a source of strength and hope for all. Archbishop Romero was beatified on 23 May 2015.

1. Make a 'Fact File' on Archbishop Oscar Romero.

2. a) Why did Oscar Romero challenge the Government?
   b) What did he do?
   c) He knew his life was in danger. Was he right to risk it?
      Give thoughtful reasons for your answer.

Martin Luther King (1929 – 1968)

Martin Luther King was a black Baptist minister. He was a prophetic voice for all the black people in America who were being treated as second-class citizens. He dreamed of a better world and worked hard to create it. As a Christian, he saw his work as a mission from God.

In many southern states of the USA, black Americans were segregated (kept apart) from white people. They had to go to separate schools, sit in different parts of buses and restaurants, use different toilets and water fountains. Many black people did not have the right to vote.

Pause to discuss

What did Jesus say about the way we should treat others that would have inspired Martin Luther King?

Civil Rights

Martin Luther King led a civil rights movement to change these injustices regarding sectarianism. Thousands of people, black and white, young and old, joined him in protest marches and suffered the violence that was used against them. They were beaten and kicked, had police dogs and fire hoses turned on them. Many were arrested and put in prison. Martin Luther King told his supporters to stand up for what was right. However, no matter what happened, they were never to use violence. He reminded them of what Jesus said:

"Love your enemies. Bless those who curse you.
Pray for those who treat you badly."

In 1963, Martin Luther King led a march to Washington DC demanding freedom and jobs.

A vast crowd heard his most inspiring speech:

"I have a dream that one day men will rise up
and come to see that they are made to live together as brothers.

I still have a dream this morning that one day every Negro in this country,
every coloured person in the world,
will be judged on the basis of the content of his character
rather than on the colour of his skin,
and every man will respect the dignity and worth of human personality.

I still have a dream today
that one day justice will roll down like water
and righteousness like a mighty stream.

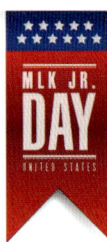

The struggle for civil rights was successful. Segregation was made illegal. Black people won the right to vote. The laws changed but some people still had hatred in their hearts. Martin Luther King was shot and killed by a white racist in 1968. He gave his life in the struggle for equality. His birthday on 15 January is now a public holiday in the United States.

Activities

1. Draw a dream cloud and write your own dream about 'justice' starting with Martin Luther King's words 'I have a dream…'

2. Discuss how Martin Luther King's faith and courage changed the lives of many.
   Mention:
   - his religious beliefs,
   - the courage he showed,
   - the unjust situations and how he responded to them,
   - how the situation for black people has now changed.

3. In the world today there are still situations of conflict and injustice.
   a) Reflect on the faith, hope, love and courage of Oscar Romero and Martin Luther King.
   b) Choose a situation of conflict or injustice. Explain what it is.
   c) Give examples of how you think either Oscar Romero or Martin Luther King would act if they were here today.

Overcoming Injustice

The Gospel Message

"Go out to the whole world and proclaim the Good News" (Mk 16:15).

In different parts of the world, there are many people who have responded to Jesus' call to go out and proclaim the Good News.

- **JUSTICE** for the poor
- **COMPASSION** for the weak

The Miracle of Madagascar

Fr. Pedro Opeka grew up in Argentina. His father was a bricklayer. When Pedro was only nine, he learned how to make bricks for building houses. At fifteen, he hesitated between becoming a professional footballer and a priest. Eventually, he decided to become a priest and joined the Vincentian Religious Order.

In September 1975, he was ordained and sent to a parish in the southeast of Madagascar. In 1989, he was sent to Antananarivo, the capital city. When he arrived, he was shocked to see the very poorest of the poor, including mothers with small children, competing with stray dogs and hundreds of rats scrabbling

in the garbage to find something to eat or some discarded things they could sell. They were surrounded by millions of flies and an unbearable smell. Fr. Pedro knew that no human being should be allowed to suffer in this way.

Trusting in God, Fr. Pedro borrowed some money and managed to buy some land. Seventy of the 'garbage people' joined him in helping to build a small farming community. Then Fr. Pedro managed to secure donations to buy food, seeds and tools. Wooden houses were quickly built and seeds planted. They had one hall which was the school.

Their little village was named Akamasoa, meaning 'community of good friends'. Little by little, these rejected people learned to trust Pedro.

Now every Sunday, Fr. Pedro celebrates Mass for thousands of people in a sports stadium.

Pause to discuss

Twenty-five years later 2016, Akamasoa has:

- 18 attractive villages,
- a population of 25,000,
- 12,000 children in primary and secondary schools,
- 59 Akamasoa primary schools, 4 middle schools, 2 high schools and a training college.

1. Watch www.madagascar-foundation.org or the PPPs (WTL DVD ROM 6).
   Make notes about what you admire most about the mission of Fr. Pedro.

2. Where do you think Fr Pedro found the courage to start this work?
   What can we learn from him?

3. **"My mission is to serve the poorest and the neediest –
   in this I found the meaning of life."** Fr. Pedro
   List the reasons why you think Fr. Pedro found the
   meaning of life in serving the poor.
   Think about:

   • Scripture text Jn 15:13 and Matt Matt 25:35-40,
   • the challenges he faced,
   • how he had to help the people to trust him and
     one another,
   • the way he had to teach the people new things and work hard,
   • the possible difficulties that had to be overcome.

4. When Pedro Opeka was fifteen, he had the choice
   of being a professional footballer or a priest.
   a) Do you think he made the right decision?
   b) Give three thoughtful reasons to support your
      opinion.

5. Research Project
   Work in groups. Choose an agency and make a display of its work.
   Explain what it does and how it puts the teaching of Jesus into practice.

Matt 25:35-40	Lk 10:29-37	Jn 15:12

   Group 1: Catholic Agency for Oversees Development - www.cafod.org.uk
   Group 2: Aid to the Church in need - www.acnuk.org
   Group 3: Catholic Mission Charity - www.missio.org.uk
   Group 4: Another charity that the school supports

Power in Weakness

Understand that we are all called to help one another.
Reflect on how people with disabilities can help us.

Helping people with disabilities

Jean Vanier is a person with a very big heart who lives out the teaching of Jesus in a radical way. He has dedicated his life to helping people, young and old, who have intellectual disabilities. He believes they are amongst the loneliest and most rejected in the world. They feel unwanted and unloved. Jean knows Jesus loves them, but they feel rejected by many people because they are 'different'. To Jean, they are 'special'.

In August 1964, Jean bought an old house in France and called it L'Arche (The Ark). It soon became a warm, loving community for 'special' people. It was not long before Jean noticed that those who came to help the people with disabilities were being helped by them. These helpers were learning to see the value and the beauty of those who have been pushed aside, humiliated and made to feel they have no value. We all have our limitations: sometimes we think we are great, but we can be selfish and arrogant. We must remember that in the eyes of God we are all equal. We are all brothers and sisters and Jesus asks us to love and help one another.

Manesh was living on the streets when he was rescued as a young child and welcomed into one of the L'Arche communities. He had suffered both physically and psychologically. It took a long time for him to be able to trust anyone because of his past experiences.

Eventually, Manesh realised that he was loved and that L'Arche was his home. He began to paint pictures and he was helped to develop this gift. At a large international meeting for L'Arche, his paintings were used to decorate the stage.

Without people to help him to develop this gift, Manesh would never have been able to make this wonderful contribution to the meeting and others would not have enjoyed the art work.

The **mission of L'Arche** is to make known the gifts of people with learning disabilities. Community life is not just sharing a home. It is making the choice to give your time to building relationships within that home. At times it will be hard, but when you experience joy and friendship with others and with God, you will not want anything else.

Now there are 147 L'Arche Communities in different parts of the world. Their shared life opens new paths of friendship between people with intellectual disabilities and those who help them in sharing daily life together.

37

Activities

1. What is the teaching of Jesus that Jean Vanier is putting into practice?

| Matt 5:7 | Jn 13:34-35 | Matt 25:35 | Lk 9:48 |

L'ARCHE
COMMUNAUTES FONDEES
PAR JEAN VANIER

2. In what ways do you think the people with intellectual disabilities are helping those who help them?

3. Why do you think this symbol was chosen for the L'Arche Communities? Try to think of three reasons.

4. Work in pairs. Imagine you are in charge of a L'Arche Community.
   You need a helper.
   a) What qualities would you look for in the person you appoint? Why?
   b) What type of person would you not accept? Why?

Preparing the Way for Jesus

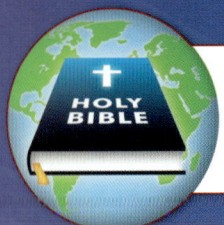

Know that Advent is a time when we prepare
to celebrate the birthday of Jesus.
Reflect on ways to prepare in this season.

The Annunciation

For some weeks now, we have been studying many aspects of justice and injustice. We have heard of the wonderful examples of people who have dedicated their lives to helping the poor, the destitute, the lonely and the unloved.

Now we are going back in time to reflect on what it is that inspires, influences and drives people to dedicate their lives to helping others. It is the great mystery of God coming down to earth, as a very humble person. He comes as a servant showing God's love, mercy, forgiveness and healing to all who earnestly seek help.

This dramatic event begins with the visit of the angel Gabriel to Mary. Mary was a

young Jewish girl living in the village of Nazareth. At that time, she was unknown, living a very humble life. Like all Jews, she was looking forward to the day when the Messiah would come.

Through the angel Gabriel, God broke into Mary's life. Mary's response to the angel is one of real faith. She is ready to let go of all her plans in order to let God be God in her life. **"I am the handmaid of the Lord,"** she says. **"Let what you have said be done to me."**

Activity

a) **Use the Bible**. Read 'The Annunciation' (Lk 1:26-38).
b) How did Mary's belief in God shape her life?
   Think about
   - What was going to happen to Mary?
   - What was so wonderful about Mary's reply to God's request?

The Visitation

Mary set out as quickly as she could to go to a town in the hill country of Judah to visit Elizabeth. "Now as soon as Elizabeth heard Mary's greeting, the child

leapt in her womb and Elizabeth was filled with the Holy Spirit. She gave a loud cry and said, 'Of all women you are the most blessed, and blessed is the fruit of your womb. Why should I be honoured with a visit from the mother of my Lord? For the moment your greeting reached my ears, the child in my womb leapt for joy'" (Lk 1:39-44).

Pause to discuss

- Who was it that inspired Elizabeth to understand what was happening?
- Why do you think Elizabeth referred to Mary as the 'Mother of my Lord'?

Mary's joy

Mary is bubbling with joy because she realises that God is going to be able to work in and through her to fulfil the promise he made to Abraham, Moses, David and all the prophets. She may not fully understand it, but she knows she has been chosen by God to give birth to the Son of God.

Pause to reflect

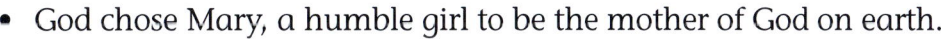

- God chose Mary, a humble girl to be the mother of God on earth.
- Mary's heart was open and yearning to receive God's love and grace. This is why she was filled with this Good News, while those full of their own importance were sent away empty.
- Through Mary, God has turned the priorities of the world upside down.

The Magnificat: Mary's song of joy

"My soul proclaims the greatness of the Lord,
my spirit rejoices in God my Saviour.
He looks on His servant in her lowliness;
from this day on all generations will
call me blessed.

The Almighty works marvels for me.
Holy is His name.
His mercy is from age to age,
on those who fear Him.
He puts forth His arm in strength
and scatters the proud-hearted.

He has cast down the mighty from their
thrones,
and raises the lowly.
He fills the hungry with good things,
sends the rich away empty.

He protects Israel, His servant,
remembering His mercy,
the mercy promised to our fathers,
to Abraham and his children forever"
(Lk 1:46-55).

Pause to discuss

- What does Mary's song of joy teach us?
- What are the qualities that God looks for in each person?
- What might happen to those who fill their hearts with many things and have no time for God?

ADVENT

This is the time when we make special preparation for the coming of God to earth and to welcome Him into our hearts.

Advent is a time when we **STOP**, **THINK** and **REFLECT** on:
- who Jesus is for us,
- how we can prepare to celebrate his birthday.

Advent is a season when we make a big effort to look at the way we:
- help one another,
- help to promote peace and justice in our homes and at school.

Advent is a time when we:
- make a special place for God in our lives;
- spend time alone with Him in prayer;
- ask God to come into our lives in a special way;
- celebrate the Sacrament of Reconciliation.

Activities

1. Think, Pair, Share
   a) What is Advent?
   b) Why is it important?
   c) How should we be preparing?
   d) What frequently happens during Advent?
   e) What do the big shops prompt us to do?
   f) What do you think are the motives of the owners of big shops?
   g) What must we try to avoid during Advent? Why?

2. **ADVENT** is a time to **STOP**, **THINK** and **REFLECT**
   Imagine you have been invited by the local radio station to give a talk about Advent. Write your script.
   Mention:
   - the advantages of taking time to **STOP**, **THINK** and **REFLECT**,
   - who is likely to benefit and why.

3. Plan a Carol Service to draw peoples' attention to the real meaning of Christmas.

The Mystery of the Incarnation

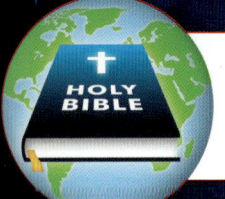

Know about the Mystery of the Incarnation
Reflect on its importance for us.

The Incarnation

In the birth of Jesus, the eternal, all-powerful and all-knowing God came to earth as a little baby. This is a very great mystery: Jesus, truly God and truly human came down to earth.

Use your Bible:

Slowly and thoughtfully read about the Birth of Jesus (Lk 2:1-20).

Pause to reflect on the importance of the birth of Jesus for us.

The Saviour of the world came, but there was no room for him.

Jesus was born in a stable.

Mary, his mother, laid him in a manger; a manger in which animals find their food.

It is this unimportant and helpless little baby who is truly the powerful one.

The first to witness this event are shepherds in a field; the poor and the despised. At first, they were terrified but the angel said, "Do not be afraid. Listen, I bring you news of great joy for all people. **Today a Saviour has been born who is Christ the Lord**".

The shepherds left their flocks and ran to find Jesus, the Lord. Then, without delay, they spread the Good News.

Worldly power threatened

King Herod was visited by wise men from the East who had seen the star over Bethlehem. He wanted to know more about this baby king.

Fear gripped Herod.

Use the Bible. Read 'The visit of the Magi' (Matt 2:1-9).

"When the wise men saw the child and Mary his mother, they fell down and worshipped him. Then, opening their treasures, they offered him gifts of gold, frankincense and myrrh. And being warned in a dream not to return to Herod, they departed to their own country by another way" (Matt 9-12).

Read 'The flight into Egypt' (Matt 2:13-15).

Before Jesus was able to walk or talk, he became a refugee. For Mary and Joseph, it seemed as if their world had turned upside down. In many ways, they were experiencing the suffering of people today.

Activities

1. Find the evidence for the following in the Gospels of Matthew and Luke; quote and give the reference:
   - Jesus was born a poor, homeless child.
   - King Herod plotted to assassinate him.
   - With his parents, he had to seek asylum in Egypt.

2. Watch PPP: The Mystery of the Incarnation (DVD ROM 6).
   For many people the true meaning of Christmas has been lost.
   It is overtaken by the ideas of presents, holidays and celebrating.
   Work in small groups.

   a) Decide on ways to help family and friends to reflect on what Christmas is really about.
   b) Share your plan with the class.
   c) Put it into action and write a report about it.

3. Exploring the Mass

Know that Jesus is the bread of life.
Think about what this means for us.

The Bread of Life

One day, Jesus said to the people,

"I am the bread of life.
He who comes to me will never be hungry;
he who believes in me will never thirst"
(Jn 6:35).

Jesus wanted the people to understand that they not only needed food such as bread to satisfy their physical hunger, but that they also needed nourishment to satisfy their spiritual hunger. Jesus is the **bread of life** because he himself is the spiritual nourishment we need for our souls, for our inner selves to grow strong.

How can Jesus be the bread of life for us?

When we read or listen to a scripture text and meditate on it, we will discover what Jesus is saying in it to help us.

Jesus will guide us when we make time to be alone with him. We invite him into our hearts to share our thoughts and listen we to him.

In a special way, Jesus is the bread of life when we receive him in Holy Communion.

In all of these ways, Jesus is the bread of life nourishing our spiritual life. Remember that Jesus is always there for us.

Pause to discuss (PPP Spiritual & Physical Needs DVD ROM 6).

- What do you think is the difference between our physical needs and our spiritual needs? Give examples.
- Why do you think we have physical needs?
- Why do you think we have spiritual needs?
- Why is it important to nourish our bodies?
- Why is it important to nourish our souls?
- In what ways do you think a friendship with Jesus can nourish our souls?

The miracle of the loaves

In order to help the people to understand what he meant by saying, "**I am the bread of life**", Jesus worked an extraordinary miracle. It showed that he could satisfy *not only* our **physical need** for food *but also* our **spiritual hunger**.

"Jesus went off to the other side of the Sea of Galilee and a large crowd followed him, impressed by the signs he had given them by curing the sick. Jesus climbed the hillside. He sat down there with his disciples. It was shortly before the Jewish feast of Passover.

Looking up, Jesus saw the crowds approaching and said to Philip, 'Where can we buy some bread for these people to eat?' He only said this to test Philip; he himself knew exactly what he was going to do. Philip answered, 'Two hundred denarii would only buy enough to give them a small piece each'. One of his disciples, Andrew, Simon Peter's

brother, said, 'There is a small boy here with five barley loaves and two fish; but what is that among so many?' Jesus said to them, 'Make the people sit down'. There was plenty of grass there, and as many as five thousand people sat down. Then Jesus took the loaves, gave thanks, and gave them out to all who were sitting ready; then he did the same with the fish, giving out as much as they wanted.

When they had eaten enough, Jesus said to the disciples, 'Pick up the pieces left over, so that nothing gets wasted'. So they picked them up, and filled twelve baskets with scraps left over from the meal of five barley loaves. The people, seeing this sign that he had given, said, 'This really is the prophet who is to come into the world'" (Jn 6:1-14).

Pause to discuss

What do you think Jesus wanted the people to understand from this miracle?

The next day, puzzled and curious, the people went looking for Jesus. He knew why they had come and said to them,

"I tell you most solemnly, you are not looking for me because you have seen the signs, but because you had all the bread you wanted to eat. Do not work for food that cannot last, but work for food that endures to eternal life" (Jn 6:26-27).

Sometimes Jesus exaggerated to make a point. He did not really expect people to stop working to provide food for themselves and their families. Jesus was trying to make them understand that they needed spiritual food too, which was more important because it would last forever.

Activities

1. Imagine you were there with the people who wanted to see Jesus the next day.
   a) List the reasons why you wanted to see him.
   b) What questions would you have wanted to ask him?
   c) What answers do you think he would have given to you?

2. 'Jesus is the bread of life.' Give examples of:
   a) some of our spiritual needs,
   b) ways in which you think Jesus can satisfy them.

The New Covenant

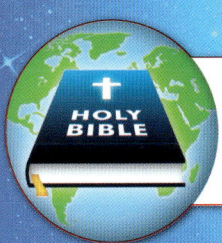

Understand that Jesus made a New Covenant with us.
Think about our part in this Covenant.

The Last Supper ➡ New Covenant

In the Old Testament, when God made a covenant with the Jews (Israelites), they agreed to live the Ten Commandments. At the Last Supper, Jesus made a **New Covenant** with us.

St. Paul tells us what happened.

"The Lord Jesus, on the night he was betrayed, took bread and when he had given thanks, he broke it, and said,

'**This is my body which is for you. Do this in remembrance of me.**' In the same way, after supper, he took the cup saying, '**This cup is the New Covenant in my blood. Do this, as often as you drink it, in remembrance of me**'.

For as often as you eat this bread and drink the cup, you proclaim the Lord's death until he comes" (1 Cor 11:23-26).

The New Covenant

At the Last Supper, Jesus made a New Covenant with his disciples and with us. He fulfilled this New Covenant by freely handing over his life in love to the Father, by accepting death on a cross. He said to his disciples and to us: **"This is my body which is handed over for you. Do this in remembrance of me."** What is Jesus asking us to do about our part in the New Covenant? Jesus is asking us to hand over our lives to him by living out this New Commandment:

The New Commandment
"I give you a New Commandment:
love one another;
just as I have loved you,
you must also love one another"
(Jn 13:34).

Pause to discuss

- At the Last Supper, what did Jesus do for us?
- How do we know?
- What is he asking us to do?
- Give examples of how we can enter into this New Covenant with him.
- How can we live out this New Covenant in daily life?

1. Imagine you have to explain what happened at the Last Supper to children preparing for their First Holy Communion.
   Make a presentation or write down what you would say to them.
   Mention what happened at the Last Supper and why it is important.

2. Make a design or a thinking map to explain the New Covenant.
   Think about:
   - what Jesus says and does,
   - what he asks of us,
   - what we can do to fulfil our part in the New Covenant.

The Beginning of Mass

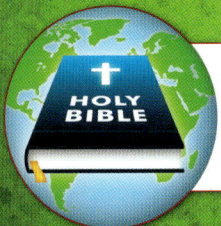

Living the New Covenant by living the New Commandment

It is at Mass in particular that we get help to live the New Covenant and New Commandment.

At the beginning of Mass, we come together to meet Jesus. The priest greets us. His greeting, 'The Lord be with you', is asking Jesus to be present with us.

The Penitential Act

In order to prepare to celebrate the Mass, the priest invites us to acknowledge our sins.

What kind of sins?

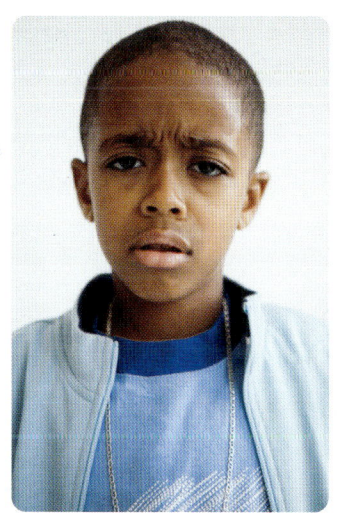

We need to think about the New Commandment Jesus has given to us. Have we truly loved God, the members of our family, everyone at school and other people? Frequently we fail to do this, so at Mass, we have the opportunity to ask God to forgive us.

At the beginning of Mass:
- we think of the sins we have committed,
- we say sorry for them,
- we ask Jesus for forgiveness.

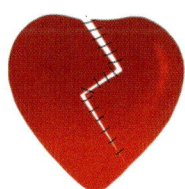

Together with all the people, we admit we have sinned and say we are sorry:

I confess to almighty God
and to you, my brothers and sisters,
that I have greatly sinned,
in my thoughts and in my words,
in what I have done and in what
I have failed to do,
through my fault, through my fault
through my most grievous fault;
therefore I ask blessed Mary ever-Virgin,
all the Angels and Saints,
and you, my brothers and sisters,
to pray for me to the Lord our God.

Activities

1. Learn the words of the 'I confess'.
   When you think you know them, test each other.

2. Divide a large circle in four.
   In each section, write an example to explain the following phrases.
   I have sinned through my own fault,
   • in my thoughts,
   • in my words,
   • in what I have done,
   • in what I have failed to do.

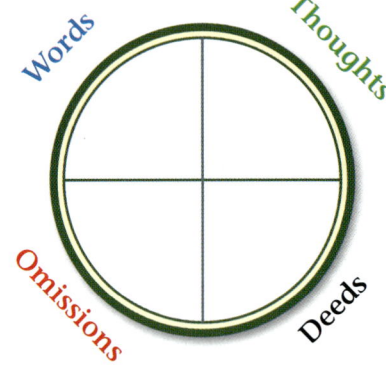

Words   Thoughts
Omissions   Deeds

The Gloria

On most Sundays and certain feast days, we sing or say the Gloria. It is a hymn of praise to God. It is a song of rejoicing in God's goodness.

Liturgy of the Word

The readings are from the Old Testament, the Letters of the New Testament and from the Gospels. These are called the **Word of God** because the writers of the Bible were inspired by God.

The words we hear in the readings are not just about what happened in the past. In them, God is speaking to us now. So we have to listen carefully, not just with our ears, but with our hearts and minds.

We cannot know what God is saying to us unless we listen to Him! Jesus says, "Blessed are those who hear the word of God and keep it" (Lk 11:28). He wants us to put into practice what we hear and understand. He wants the **Word of God** to influence what we do and say.

The Gospel

Before the reading of the Gospel the priest greets us with the words:

The Lord be with you.

We reply: *And with your spirit.*

When the priest says:

A reading from the holy Gospel according to …

We reply: *Glory to you, O Lord.*

While saying these words, it is a tradition for us to make a little cross + on our forehead, lips and heart. This is asking God to be in our thoughts (head), in our words (lips) and in our heart.

At the end of the Gospel, the priest says: *The Gospel of the Lord.*

We reply: *Praise to you, Lord Jesus Christ.*

Activities

1. The readings at Mass can help us when we are sad, lonely, tired, happy, worried, annoyed, in need of something or wanting to feel loved by God.

   a) Look up the following quotations from the Bible.

   | Jn 14:1 | Jn 14:14-15 | Lk 6:27 | Isaiah 43:4 | Col 3:12 |

   b) Choose the quotations that best fit the faces below. Draw the face and put the scripture reference with it. Give reasons for your choice.

2. a) Why is the Liturgy of the Word a very important part of the Mass?

   b) Explain how some of the readings could influence moral values and behaviour.

The Offertory at Mass

The Offertory

At the Offertory, when we see people taking the bread and wine up to the altar, we offer our lives to Jesus. The bread and the wine are symbols of our self-offering. They represent the gift we make of ourselves to God. For example, we can offer:

- the times we have helped others,
- the successes, good things that have happened,
- our disappointments and difficulties.

All these gifts are offered to God the Father when the priest says:

*Blessed are you, Lord, God of all creation,
for through your goodness we have the bread we offer you:
fruit of the earth and work of human hands,
it will become for us the bread of life.*
We reply: **Blessed be God forever.**

*Blessed are you, Lord, God of all creation,
for through your goodness we have received
the wine we offer you,
fruit of the vine and work of human hands,
it will become our spiritual drink.*
We reply: **Blessed be God forever.**

The gift of ourselves and all that we do to help others, God transforms into something beautiful. In return, we receive God's love and grace.

a) Explain what happens at the Offertory of the Mass.
   Why is it very important?
b) Give examples of the offerings we can make to Jesus.

Blessed Chiara Badano (1971-1990)

Chiara Badano offered her life to Jesus. In return, she received the love and grace of Jesus and experienced inner peace and joy.

Chiara was a young Italian girl who loved swimming, mountain climbing, ice-skating, skiing and tennis. While playing tennis, she began to complain about a pain in her shoulder. At first, it was assumed that she had strained it on the court. However, when the pain did not go away, she had an MRI scan. Chiara was told that she had a tumour in her bone; the treatment would be very severe.

She came home from hospital, threw herself on her bed and stayed there for about half an hour. In this time, Chiara made the decision to hand over her life to Jesus. She believed that whether she lived or died, she was safe in the hands of Jesus. She put all her trust in him. During the difficult months that followed, she remained very close to Jesus.

Throughout this severe illness, her friends were always amazed to find her joyful and interested in what they were doing. "She was not thinking of herself, but of us," they said.

Eleven months later, on 7 October 1990, Chiara died. She had requested that she be buried in a white dress like a bride going to meet Jesus and said, "Don't shed any tears for me. I'm going to Jesus. At my funeral, I don't want people crying, but singing with all their hearts".

1. What do you think was the secret of Chiara's joy?
   What can we learn from her?

2. In what ways do you think Chiara might be an
   inspiration to young people today?

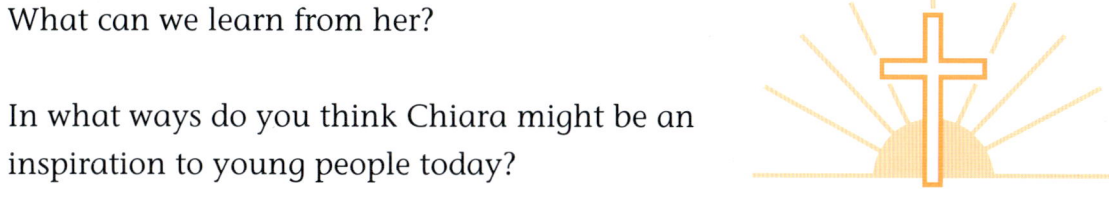

The Consecration

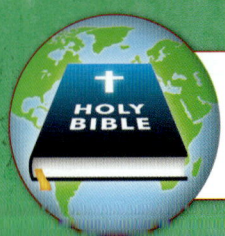

What happens at the Consecration?

At the Consecration, Jesus becomes truly present in the bread and wine. This is the way God reaches out to us. He gives Himself to us in the gift of Jesus, who is truly God and truly human.

But how do I know Jesus is present when I can't see him?
Tony

We cannot see everything that exists. We do not see our intelligence, yet we know we have it. We do not see our mind but, we can experience its effects because we can think and make decisions.

It is only by the gift of faith that we can believe in the presence of Jesus in the Eucharist. At the Last Supper, when Jesus gave the bread to the Apostles, he said, "This is my body". When he gave them the cup of wine to drink, he said, "This is my blood". Jesus can bring about what he says.

The Consecration

At the Consecration, we remember and participate in the Last Supper, which Jesus had with the Apostles before he was crucified. The miraculous change in the bread and wine is brought about by the power of the Holy Spirit.

We believe Jesus is present when the priest raises the sacred host and says,

"Take this, all of you and eat of it,
for this is my body,
which will be given up for you".

We believe Jesus is present when the chalice is raised and the priest says,

"Take this, all of you and drink from it,
for this is the chalice of my blood,
the blood of the new and eternal Covenant,
which will be poured out for you and for many
for the forgiveness of sins".

We still see bread, we still see wine, but with our faith we say, Jesus is really and truly present and he is God.

Jesus makes the perfect sacrifice

It is at the consecration in the Mass when **we remember the sacrifice** that Jesus made when he freely offered his life on the cross. He handed over his life in love to the Father as the most perfect sacrifice to take away the sins of the world. His love was so perfect that it overcame death and he rose triumphantly.

Now Jesus, in the person of the priest, offers the sacrifice of his Body and Blood and invites us to offer ourselves in thanksgiving to the Father. The priest says,

"Through him, and with him, and in him, O God, almighty Father in the unity of the Holy Spirit, all glory and honour is yours, for ever and ever."

We reply: **AMEN.**

Activities

1. Look back at Tony's question on page 54 and write an answer to it.

2. Think of a way to explain to someone who is not a Catholic what we believe about the Eucharist and why we believe it.
   You will need to make links with the Last Supper.

Holy Communion

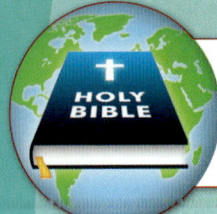

Know that it is Jesus we receive in Holy Communion.
Be aware of how important this is for us.

Our Father

In preparation for Holy Communion, we are invited to stand as
one family and pray to God our Father. It is the
same prayer that Jesus taught to the disciples.

"Our Father who art in heaven,
hallowed be thy name."
May your name always be kept holy.

"Thy Kingdom come, thy will be done on earth as it is in heaven."
May your Kingdom of love and trust come into our world.

"Give us this day our daily bread."
May you give us nourishment for our body and soul.

"Forgive us our trespasses as we forgive those who trespass against us."
May you forgive us our sins in the same way as we forgive those who hurt us.

"Lead us not into temptation, but deliver us from evil."
Do not let us be tempted to do things that are wrong.

Activities

1. How can we bring God's Kingdom into the world? Discuss.

2. Why do you think the 'Our Father' is a good preparation for Holy
   Communion? Some clues: Praise; God's will; Kingdom; Forgiveness.

3. We ask God to forgive us our sins in the same way as we forgive others.
   Give two examples to show what this really means.

Receiving Holy Communion

As we prepare to receive Jesus in Holy Communion, we remember that he is the nourishment we need for our souls, for our inner lives, because:

- **Jesus** is the **Way** to the Father.
- **Jesus** teaches us the **Truth** about life.
- **Jesus** offers us eternal **Life** with God.

When we receive Jesus in Holy Communion, we become more deeply part of him and we are given a promise of sharing his life fully in heaven.

We welcome Jesus into our hearts. The time after Holy Communion is a time of most special prayer. During it, we speak personally to Jesus who is present within us.

We have to be very careful not to be distracted by others around us. We must find our own way of focusing on the presence of Jesus within us. If we deliberately let our thoughts wander, Jesus will not give us a nudge to remind us that he is with us. It is up to us to really make an effort to be with him. He loves each of us immensely.

 Don't miss this precious opportunity to ask Jesus to help you. Share your most private thoughts with Jesus and let him know how much you love him.

 **Pause to reflect**

Think of two ways to help you remain present with Jesus when you receive Holy Communion. Write them down.

Blessing at the end of Mass

At the end of Mass, the priest gives us a blessing and we are called to live out the Mass in our daily lives.

"Go in peace, glorifying the Lord by your life."

Our mission is to fulfil our part of the New Covenant by putting into practice the New Commandment.

"I give you a New Commandment:
love one another;
just as I have loved you,
you must also love one another"
(Jn 13:34).

It is by fulfilling this New Commandment that others will know that we are truly Christians.

Activities

1. List some of the ways you can put the New Commandment into practice in your daily life.

2. Draw an outline of your hand. Look back at the parts of the Mass.
   Think about: The beginning, Readings, Offertory, Communion and final blessing.
   On each finger and the thumb write down one thing you should do to help you participate in each part of the Mass.

3. How do you think each part of the Mass will help us to live our lives more fully?
   Explain what we need to do:

   i)   at the beginning,
   ii) during the Readings,
   iii) at the Offertory,
   iv) at the Consecration,
   v) at Communion,
   vi) at the end of Mass.

4. In some countries where Catholics are not allowed to practise their faith and receive the sacraments, many of them are prepared to risk their lives to be able to celebrate Mass.
   Give reasons why you think the Mass is so important for them.
   (For help see WS TB p. 78)

The Eucharist: Source & Summit of Life

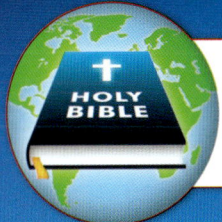

Understand that the Eucharist is the source and summit of life. Reflect on its importance for us.

Jesus is the source of life

Think of the power of electricity. When we plug in and switch on, this source of

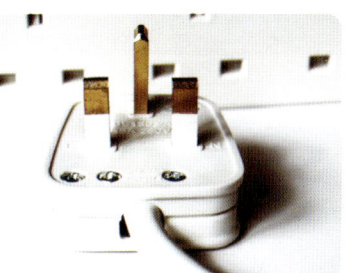

energy makes things happen: lights blaze, kettles boil, we can charge laptops and mobiles so we can find information and talk to friends. Things will happen when we 'plug in' to Jesus. He is the source of strength and energy which enables us to be fully committed Christians.

> How do we know Jesus is the source of life?
>
> Sabrina

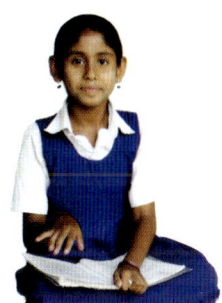

To understand what is meant by Jesus being the 'source of life', let us look again at what happened at the **Last Supper**, **Good Friday** and **Easter Sunday**.

Holy Thursday: Last Supper

At the **Last Supper**, Jesus told his disciples that he was about to **hand over** his life for us. In this way, he made a **New Covenant**. He was saying that he was going to give his life for us, and he was asking us to do the same for him.

In entering into this New Covenant with Jesus, we can be sure:

- Jesus is with us – when we are happy.
- He is with us – when we are anxious.
- He is with us – when someone hurts us.

Good Friday: Crucifixion

On the day after the Last Supper, **Good Friday**, Jesus actually handed over his life. When dying on the cross, he offered his life for each one of us.

Jesus gave himself to the Father as the most perfect sacrifice to take away the sins of the world and to open the way to heaven for us. This was the fulfilment of the **New Covenant**.

Easter Sunday: Resurrection

Three days later on **Easter Sunday**, Jesus rose to be the Lord of the living and the dead, that is, to be the **Saviour**.

Since rising from the dead, Jesus has a totally new relationship with us. He is able to share his **new life** with us. Jesus has become the **source of eternal life**.

We receive this life from him in a very special way when we celebrate the Eucharist.

What is the summit of Christian life?
Chris

The summit of Christian life

The summit of a mountain is the highest peak. So the summit of Christian life is like reaching the highest peak of our relationship with Jesus.

In celebrating the Eucharist, which we call the **Mass**, Jesus gives himself to us.

Jesus asks us to offer to him all that we do to help others. Insofar as we truly and sincerely do this, we reach the **summit of life**.

The Eucharist is the source and summit of Christian life

The **source of life** is in the Mass, when we draw spiritual strength and energy from Jesus in the Eucharist to help us to live out the values of the Kingdom of God. This is the **source** of Christian life.

The **summit of life** is when we offer the whole of our lives to Jesus in the Mass. He promises that he will always be with us to help us to live out the **New Commandment** in our daily lives.

Activities

1. Write an explanation to answer the questions asked by Sabrina and Chris. You will need to mention the following.
    a)   At the Last Supper, what did Jesus say he was going to do?
    b)   What was he asking us to do?
    c)   What did Jesus do on Good Friday?
    d)   Why did he do this?
    e)   What happened on Easter Sunday?
    f)   What is Jesus able to give to us now?
    g)   What has he become for us?

2. Identify how the Eucharist is the source and summit of Christian life. Explain how this belief has arisen.

3. Many people don't really understand why the Mass is so important. They don't understand that it is the source and summit of the whole Christian life. Make a little booklet with explanations and illustrations.
    Include:
    • Jesus as the source of life,
    • New Covenant and how we live it out,
    • participating in the Mass - the summit of life.

The Blessed Sacrament

Know that Jesus is present in the Blessed Sacrament.
Be aware of how his presence can help us.

The Blessed Sacrament

Jesus has promised to be with his Church until the end of time. One of the ways in which he fulfils this promise is through his permanent presence in the Blessed Sacrament.

To all Catholics, the Blessed Sacrament is very precious. It is what we call the consecrated hosts. These are kept in a ciborium in the tabernacle so that we can always pray in the presence of Jesus.

The Blessed Sacrament can also be taken to people who are very ill in hospital or at home and are unable to get to Mass.

Throughout the world, in every tabernacle, in every church Jesus waits for us to come to him. It is important to show reverence for Jesus in the Blessed Sacrament. While we are in church, we try to be very quiet. The sanctuary lamp is a sign that Jesus is present in the tabernacle. In reverence for the Blessed Sacrament, we genuflect towards the tabernacle when we enter and leave the church.

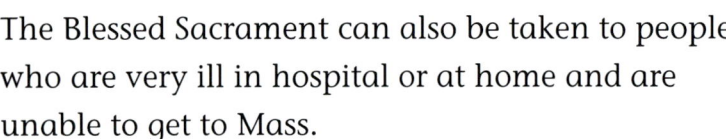

Activities

1. Choose a hymn about the Blessed Sacrament, for example, 'O Bread of Life' or 'Godhead here in hiding'.
   In what ways do the words speak to us of the presence of Jesus?

2. Write your own prayer to Jesus in the Blessed Sacrament.

Pause to reflect

A visit to the Blessed Sacrament

- Jesus is waiting for us. He knows us so well.
- We allow time for our hearts and minds to become conscious of his presence.
- We share our deepest thoughts and desires with Jesus.
- We listen to Jesus.
- We can tell him everything and anything.
- We remember that Jesus has told us to trust in God and trust in him.
- Slowly and surely we will experience his peace coming over us.

Benediction: Adoration of the Blessed Sacrament

The Blessed Sacrament is kept in the tabernacle, but when we have Benediction, it is placed on the altar in a monstrance.

Benediction is a special time of prayer, of adoring Jesus in the Blessed Sacrament.

When entering or leaving the church during Benediction, we genuflect on both knees and bow our heads in reverence.

Activities

1. With the help of the glossary, write out the meaning of the following words:
   Genuflect   **Monstrance**   **Sanctuary Lamp**   **Tabernacle**

2. Make a leaflet to encourage others to make a visit to the Blessed Sacrament in the church.
   Include:
   - what the Blessed Sacrament is and where to find it;
   - why it is helpful to make a visit;
   - a few suggestions for what a person could do during a visit.

4. Jesus the Messiah

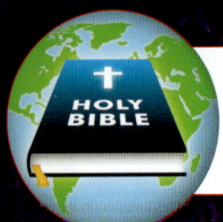

**Deepen our understanding of Jesus.
Reflect on what you believe about your faith.**

Big Questions

The pupils in St. Benedict's School have been learning about Jesus for several years, yet they still have many big questions for the teacher. They know that it is very important to be able to share with others **what** they believe about their faith and **why** they believe it.

How do we know that Jesus is truly God?
Anna

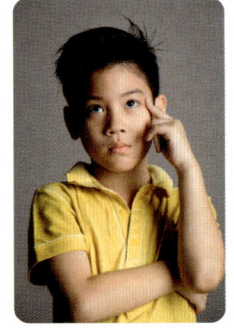

Why did Jesus have to die on a cross?
Ben

How do we know that Jesus is truly human?
Luc

Why did Jesus make a New Covenant with us?
Sophie

Why did some of the Jewish authorities not like Jesus?
Rasha

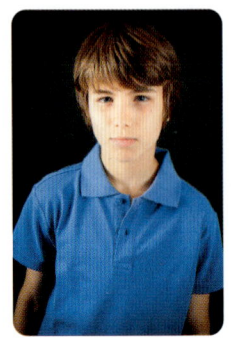

When Jesus was arrested, couldn't he have worked a miracle and escaped?
Carlo

Questions and Answers

Miss Smith knew that she had already explained some of the questions that the pupils were asking, so it was time to get them to do research in the Bible and look back on what they had studied.

Activities

1. **How do we know Jesus is truly God and truly human?**

   a) Work in small groups. For evidence, research:

Lk 2:5-7	Lk 2:51-52	Lk 8:23	Lk 24:42-43
Mk 2:1-12	Mk 1:40-45	Mk 3:1-6	Mk 7:31-37

   b) Use this evidence to answer the question. It can be a speech, a diagram or Power Point presentation.

   > Why did Jesus make a New Covenant with us?

2. Let us go back to look at the reasons for the New Covenant.

   a) What do you know about Adam and Eve?

   b) What happened when they disobeyed God?

   c) What were the effects of their first sin?

   d) How did God continue to help them?

   e) With whom did God make a covenant?

   f) What did God give the Israelites to help them?

   g) Eventually, who did God send to help the people?

   h) Why did God send Jesus?

   i) Why did Jesus make a New Covenant with us?

3. **Why did the Pharisees, scribes and Sadducees not like Jesus?**

Here are some reasons why the religious authorities objected to what Jesus was doing.

  i) This man Jesus mixes with outcasts and sinners.
  ii) He heals people on the Sabbath Day.
  iii) His disciples do not follow our customs about washing and eating.
  iv) He teaches new things about the Law on his own authority.
  v) He claims to forgive sins – something that only God can do.
  vi) His disciples gather grain on the Sabbath.

Use these references to link the reasons with the evidence.

Mk 2:15–17   **Mk 2:23–3:6**   **Mk 2:4–7**   **Mk 7:1–5**

4.   a) What do you think the religious authorities feared most of all about Jesus?
     b) Were they right to fear him? Why or why not?

Death on a cross – why?

When Jesus was arrested, couldn't he have worked a miracle and escaped?

Why did Jesus have to die on the cross?

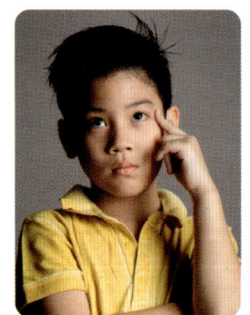

The Jewish authorities demanded the crucifixion of Jesus because they considered him a law-breaker. Pilate finally gave in to their demand and so Jesus had to die on the cross.

When Jesus was condemned to death, he **chose** not to work a miracle and escape. He freely offered his life on the cross for our salvation. His death and resurrection bring us eternal life.

Identity of Jesus

**Understand that Jesus is the Messiah.
Be aware of what this means for us.**

Who is Jesus?

Jesus knew that the time was coming for him to go to Jerusalem and to suffer grievously at the hands of the religious authorities, to be put to death and to be raised to life on the third day.

The Transfiguration

To strengthen the faith of Peter, James and John by revealing to them his true identity, Jesus led them up a high mountain where they could be alone.

"There, in their presence, he was transfigured: his face shone like the sun and his clothes became as white as the light.

Suddenly Moses and Elijah appeared to them; they were talking with Jesus. Then Peter spoke to Jesus, 'Lord,' he said, 'it is wonderful for us to be here; if you wish, I will make three tents here, one for you, one for Moses and one for Elijah.' He was still speaking when suddenly a bright cloud covered them with shadow, and from the cloud, there came a voice which said, '**This is my Son, the Beloved; he enjoys my favour. Listen to him.**' When they heard this, the disciples fell on their faces, overcome with fear. But Jesus came up and touched them. 'Stand up,' he said, 'do not be afraid.' And when they raised their eyes, they saw no one but only Jesus" (Matt 17:2-8).

The Transfiguration reveals that **Jesus is the Messiah**. The dazzling brightness which shone out from his body showed his divinity, that he was truly God.

Moses and Elijah who appeared were Old Testament prophets. They did what God asked of them. Now, it is only **Jesus** who **has authority** over people in the world.

The Transfiguration confirmed that the **Kingdom of the Messiah would be glorious**. The three disciples were given a preview of the glory of Jesus.

A very important point was that Jesus wanted his disciples to know that he would be glorified, but it would not be the kind of glory that people were expecting. He was not going to be their powerful warrior to drive out the Romans who occupied their country.

His **glory** would come about through his **Passion**, **Death** and **Resurrection**.

Suffering was the path to glory. This was very puzzling for Peter, James and John. They had to unlearn what they had always believed and learn a new way of thinking which is that **God's ways are not our ways**. Very often, **God's ways are mysterious**.

Pause to discuss

Imagine you were with Peter, James and John.

- What do you think were their hopes and fears?
- What questions would you have wanted to ask Jesus?
- Why do you think Moses was there with Jesus?
- Can you explain in what way suffering was the path to glory for Jesus?

Fears and suspicion grow …

One day, the Jews gathered around Jesus and said to him, 'How long will you keep us in suspense? If you are the Messiah, tell us plainly'. Jesus replied, '**I have told you and you do not believe**'. The Jews were angry and took up stones to throw at him because they believed that what he said was blasphemy; he was making himself God. They tried to arrest him but Jesus escaped (cf. Jn 10:24-39).

All eyes on Jesus

Jesus received word that his friend Lazarus, the brother of Martha and Mary, was seriously ill. Two days later, when he arrived at Bethany, Lazarus had already died. All eyes were on Jesus. What did they think he was going to do?

Activities

1. **Use your Bible.** Read the 'Death of Lazarus' (Jn 11:17-48).
   a) In what way did Martha show her faith in Jesus?
   b) What did Mary say to Jesus? Did she have faith in him? Why?
   c) What was it about Jesus that tells us he was truly human?
   d) What did Jesus do next?
   e) What does this tell us about him?
   f) How did the Jews react?

2. Write a play-script on the resurrection of Lazarus (Jn 11:1-44).
   Include:
   • Narrator,
   • Jesus and some disciples,
   • Martha and Mary,
   • onlookers.

3. There is evidence in abundance that Jesus is the Messiah.
   • Say what you think and why.
   • Give a different point of view and say why some people hold it.
   • Say why you disagree and quote some evidence.

4. What does our belief in Jesus as Messiah mean for us today? (Clues on pp.66 and 68)

Journey to Jerusalem

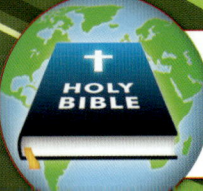

**Know about the final journey Jesus made to Jerusalem.
Reflect on the thoughts and feelings of Jesus.**

Holy Week

Holy Week is the most important week in the year for Christians. It is known as 'Holy Week' because it lasts from Passion (Palm) Sunday to Holy Saturday. All over the world, Christians re-live the events which happened over 2,000 years ago. In all our churches, we carry palms to remember the triumphant journey of Jesus to Jerusalem. We are now going to re-live the most dramatic, earth shattering and amazing events day by day in the life of Jesus.

The Messiah enters Jerusalem

Jesus and his disciples set out for Jerusalem. When they were approaching the Mount of Olives, Jesus said to two of them, "Go off to the village facing you, and as soon as you enter it, you will find a tethered colt (a young donkey), that no one has yet ridden. Untie it and bring it here. If anyone says to you, 'What are you doing?' say, 'The Master needs it and he will send it back here directly'.

The disciples took the colt to Jesus and threw their cloaks on its back, and he sat on it. Many people spread their cloaks on the road, others greenery which they had cut in the fields. Those who went in front and those who followed were all shouting, **Hosanna! Blessings on him who comes in the name of the Lord"** (Mk 11:2-9).

The people thought that Jesus was going to be triumphant once they reached Jerusalem. The religious leaders felt threatened and challenged by the crowds and the excitement of the people. The political leaders feared that Jesus was becoming a threat to the nation.

Pause to discuss

Study this illustration. Find the religious leaders and the politicians.

- What do you think the religious leaders were saying to one another?
- Were they right to feel threatened? Give reasons.
- What reasons might the political leaders have had for fearing Jesus?
- How do you think Jesus was feeling? Why?
- Imagine you were with the disciples. What do you think might happen next? Why?

Activities

1. You are a reporter on the **Jerusalem News**. You have been sent to cover the arrival of Jesus of Nazareth in Jerusalem.
   a) Describe the scene and report on what some of the people involved said.
   b) Give your opinion on what you think is likely to happen next.

2. As Jesus entered Jerusalem, he knew that many people expected a Messiah who would be king and drive out the Romans.
   Outline what you think were his feelings, thoughts and plans for the days ahead.

Holy Thursday

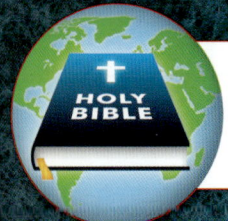

Know about the events of Holy Thursday.
Reflect on the importance of these events for us.

Plot to betray Jesus

Three days after the triumphal entry of Jesus and the disciples into Jerusalem, "Judas Iscariot, one of the Twelve, approached the chief priests with an offer to hand Jesus over to them. They were delighted to hear it, and promised to give him money; and he looked for a way of betraying him when the opportunity should occur" (Mk 14:10-11). Since then, this day of Holy Week is often called **Spy Wednesday**.

Holy Thursday: Jesus washes the feet of the disciples

"It was before the festival of the Passover, and Jesus knew that the hour had come for him to pass from this world to the Father. He had always loved those who were his own in the world, but now he showed how perfect his love was. They were at supper and the devil had already put it into the mind of Judas Iscariot son of Simon, to betray him" (Jn 13:1-2).

Jesus got up from table, "removed his outer garment and, taking a basin and towel, wrapped it round his waist; he then poured water into a basin and began to wash the disciples' feet and to wipe them with the towel he was wearing" (Jn 13:4-5).

The disciples were shocked at this! However, Jesus was trying to teach them a very important lesson.

This lesson was that Jesus, the **Messiah**, was doing the work of the lowest servant. He did not claim any status for himself or high position as Lord and Master. Jesus said to them, **"I have given you an example so that you may copy what I have done"** (Jn 13:15). Jesus is not asking us to wash each other's feet, but he is asking us to always think of ways we can be helpful and kind to others.

Pause to discuss

a) When Jesus washed the feet of the disciples, what was the most important lesson they had to learn from it?

b) Give an example of how we can put this lesson into practice.

c) In what way does this lesson link to the New Commandment?

The treachery of Judas foretold

After washing their feet, Jesus was troubled in spirit and declared, "I tell you most solemnly, one of you will betray me". The disciples looked at one another, wondering who he meant. Peter nudged John to ask him. Jesus replied, "The one to whom I give the piece of bread that I shall dip in the dish". He dipped the piece of bread and gave it to Judas (cf. Jn 13:21-26).

Judas took the bread and slipped away. The others thought he had gone to buy something they needed for the festival or to give money to the poor. The truth was, Judas was about to accept the bribe the religious authorities offered. In return for it, he would tell them where Jesus would be and how they could arrest him.

Pause to reflect

- What do you think were the thoughts in the mind of Jesus when Judas left the table?
- Why do you think Judas decided to betray Jesus? Do you think he had thought through the consequences? Why or why not?

The Garden of Gethsemane

When they had finished the **Last Supper**, Jesus went with his disciples to the Garden of Gethsemane on the Mount of Olives.

Jesus knew that Judas had gone out to betray him and he was very distressed.

He went a little way off from his disciples and knelt down to pray, **"My Father, if it be possible let this cup pass from me, nevertheless, let it be, not as I, but as you would have it"** (Matt 26:39). The 'cup' that Jesus mentions is the suffering he is about to undergo.

When he rose from prayer, Jesus went to the disciples and found them asleep. And he said to Peter, **"So you have not the strength to keep awake with me one hour"** (Matt 26:40).

Jesus knew what lay ahead of him and he accepted it willingly. But here in the garden, he felt totally alone. He had asked Peter, James and John to watch and pray with him, but they had fallen asleep.

Jesus is arrested

It was at this moment that Judas arrived with armed men carrying swords and clubs. They seized Jesus and took him to the high priest's palace.

Use the Bible. Read Matt 26:47-56.

a) What did Judas do?

b) What did one of the other disciples do?

c) What did Jesus say to this disciple?

d) What does this tell us about Jesus?

e) How do we know that Jesus freely accepted this suffering?

f) What did Jesus say to the crowds?

g) Why do you think Jesus reminded them of the scriptures and the prophets?

h) When Jesus was led away, what did the disciples do?

i) What does it tell us about the disciples?

The Trial before the Sanhedrin (PPP on DVD ROM 6)

Laws for Trials

- Jewish trials had to be held during the hours of daylight.
- Two independent witnesses had to agree on their evidence; if not, the defendant had to be acquitted.
- The High Priest sat in judgement but could not ask any incriminating questions.

Activities

1. **Use the Bible.** Read Matt 26:59-68
   - Re-read the laws for Trials above.
   - Did Jesus have a fair trial?
   - Support your views with evidence from Scripture.

2. "**At the Trial, Jesus provoked the Sanhedrin and deserved to be condemned to death.**" Discuss.
   Read Matt 26:59-68.
   - Say what you think and why.
   - Give a different point of view and say why others hold it.
   - Say why you disagree with it and quote the evidence.

3. Write a diary account of what it must have been like for Peter on Holy Thursday.
   Read Matt 26:36-41 and 69-75.
   Mention:
   - Garden of Gethsemane,
   - the courtyard,
   - the cock crowing,
   - how he was feeling,
   - evidence to show he had courage,
   - evidence to show he loved Jesus.

4. Imagine you are Peter's friend. Write to him; show understanding for his behaviour. Encourage him to rise to the challenges of being a disciple.

Good Friday

Know about the crucifixion of Jesus.
Reflect on what it was like for Mary and the disciples.

Trial before Pontius Pilate

As soon as daylight broke, the religious authorities took Jesus to Pontius Pilate. "Pilate questioned Jesus, 'Are you the king of the Jews?' 'It is you who say it', Jesus answered. The chief priests

brought many accusations against him. Pilate questioned him again, 'Have you no reply at all? See how many accusations they are bringing against you!' But, to Pilate's amazement, Jesus made no further reply.

At festival time, it was the custom to release a prisoner. Pilate asked the people if they wanted him to release the king of the Jews. He realised that it was out of jealousy that the chief priests had handed him over. But the chief priests had encouraged the people to demand the release of Barabbas instead. Barabbas was a terrorist and had committed murder during an uprising.

When Pilate brought both of these men forward, he asked the crowd who they wanted released. They shouted, 'Barabbas!' They called for Jesus to be crucified. 'Why?' Pilate asked them. 'What harm has he done?' But they shouted all the louder, 'Crucify him!'

Pilate, anxious to please the crowd, released Barabbas for them and having ordered Jesus to be scourged, handed him over to be crucified" (Mk 15:1-15).

 The soldiers led Jesus away. They twisted some thorns into a crown and pressed it on his head. Then they saluted him, 'Hail, king of the Jews!' They struck his head with a reed and spat on him. When they had finished making fun of him, they led him away to crucify him.

Pause to discuss

- Why did the Jewish religious authorities bring Jesus to Pilate?
- What do you think Pilate wanted to do with Jesus?
- Eventually, what did Pilate do to Jesus? Why?
- Were his reasons justified? Why or why not?
- What does it tell us about Pilate's character?

The disciples

The disciples knew they had let Jesus down; they knew they were cowards. They were afraid of what would happen to them. The hopes they had of their Master being the Messiah were shattered. The miracles they had witnessed were forgotten – what use were they now that he was dead?

Pause to reflect

Think of the suffering Jesus experienced.

Jesus felt terror and loneliness in the Garden of Gethsemane.

He was arrested at night, after being betrayed by one of his own disciples.

 He had to suffer the complete desertion of his disciples.

He had to face unjust trials.

He was spat on.

He was beaten and flogged.

He was forced to carry his own cross.

He was crucified.

He was buried in a borrowed tomb.

Holy Saturday

Mary spent Holy Saturday in trust and patience. She contemplated the mystery of God's plan. She knew that God's ways are mysterious and it was vital to keep trusting in Him.

Even though her heart must have been pierced with suffering, Mary was able to help the confused disciples. She remembered all that God had done for her and she hoped in Him.

Mary looked back on her life with Jesus and held on to her total trust in God's promises.

Activities

1. a) What different types of 'hurt' can you identify in the reflection on page 78?
   b) Which type do you feel is the most hurtful? Why?
   c) Think about the suffering that Mary, his mother, experienced on Good Friday. Write a reflection or poem on it.

2. Look back on Mary's life. What were the events that she was now able to recall to help her to continue to trust and hope in God? Clues:

| Lk 1:31-32 | Lk 1:41-43 | Lk 1:46-49 | Lk 2:17-19 | Lk 2:33-35 |

3. Write a homily or a poem on trust, joys and sufferings in Mary's life.

Pause to reflect

"The Cross of Jesus bears the suffering and the sin of mankind, including our own. Jesus accepts all this with open arms, bearing on his shoulders our crosses and saying to us: Have courage! You do not carry your own cross alone! I carry it with you. I have overcome death and I have come to give you hope, to give you life." Pope Francis

Easter Sunday

Deepen our understanding of the Resurrection. Reflect on what the Resurrection means for us.

The Resurrection

The death of Jesus had its own 'punctuation'. It could be followed with a full stop, a question mark, an exclamation mark, or a to be continued mark.

 Some hoped it would be a full stop. They thought that killing Jesus would be the end of the matter.

 For some, the death of Jesus was a question mark. Some of his followers couldn't quite accept that Jesus was finished. Yet, they could not understand why it had happened.

 For many of his followers, the death of Jesus came as a shocking surprise.

 And yet, Jesus knew that it was not the end of the story: on the third day, he would rise from the dead.

What does the Resurrection mean for us?

The resurrection of Jesus gives us hope that when we die, God will raise us up to new life. We believe we will live forever with Jesus in the Kingdom of heaven.

We believe the Risen Jesus is always close to us. His Spirit is alive within us and he is looking after us. Also, if we believe in him, he offers deep inner peace. He is **the Way, the Truth and the Life** for us (Jn 14:6).

Accounts of the Resurrection

1. For each account of the Resurrection,
   a) use a Bible to check the references below,
   b) match the reference with the number of the illustration,
   c) give the account a title and write a very brief summary of what happened.

| Jn 20:1-18 | Lk 24:36-43 | Matt 28:1-8 | Jn 20:19-29 | Jn 21:1-14 | Lk 24:13-35 |

2. In the world today, there are many people who do not know about the Resurrection of Jesus. Your task is to be his disciples. Use all modern **means** of communication to make known the events of the Resurrection.

Work in pairs or small groups. Include:

- how you are going to spread the news;
- the accounts of the Resurrection you are going to use;
- what the Resurrection means for you and will mean for others;
- the design, illustrations and images;
- the importance of praying to Jesus for the gift of faith. (Think of doubting Thomas).

Holy Week in Church

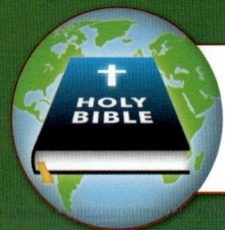

Know about the Holy Week ceremonies in church.
Reflect on their importance for us.

Passion Sunday

Passion Sunday is also known as Palm Sunday. Palm branches are blessed and the Gospel account of the entry of Jesus into Jerusalem is read. There is often a procession into church when we sing 'Hosanna'.

One of the readings at Mass is the Gospel account of the trial and death of Jesus.

Pause to reflect

When Jesus entered Jerusalem the people cheered to welcome him, *'Hosanna to the Son of David'*. Yet a few days later, these cheers turned to jeers: 'Crucify him!'

Activities

1. In what ways might this illustration help us to recall:
   a) Jesus' entry into Jerusalem,
   b) what happens in church on Passion Sunday?

2. Passion Sunday in Madagscar. (PPP on DVD ROM 6)
   Imagine you are there and some onlookers ask what is happening.
   a) Explain why so many people have come together.
   b) Tell the onlookers why you think going to church on Passion Sunday helps people. Briefly explain what happens at Mass on this day.

Holy Thursday

Mass is celebrated in the evening on **Holy Thursday**. The scripture readings are from the account of the Last Supper and Jesus washing the disciples' feet at the Last Supper. After the Gospel, the priest washes the feet of twelve people in memory of this event.

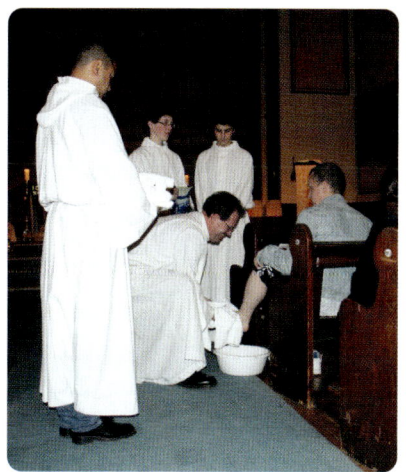

After Mass, the altar in the church is stripped bare to

remind us how Jesus was stripped of his garments before he died.

The Blessed Sacrament is carried in procession to a side-altar. Many people stay there to pray.

Pause to discuss

- What were the two most important actions that Jesus did at the Last Supper? (1 Cor 11:23-26)
- What did Jesus ask of us?
- Why did Jesus wash the feet of his disciples?
- What is the lesson he wanted us to learn from this action?
- What do you think are the main reasons why people would want to stay in the presence of the Jesus on Holy Thursday night?

Activities

1. a) What are the **Stations of the Cross**? (PPP on DVD ROM 6).
   b) Why do you think people make the Stations of the Cross?
   c) In what ways might they help people who are suffering?

2. Think of a way to help younger pupils understand what happened at the Last Supper and how this event is re-lived in church on Holy Thursday. For example, make a diagram, podcast or a Power Point presentation. You need to include:
   - the New Covenant,
   - the New Commandment,
   - how they link with the Holy Thursday liturgy.

Good Friday

The altar is bare and the tabernacle empty. As the priest comes in, he prostrates in front of the altar as a sign of humility, and of grief and sorrow at the suffering of Jesus.

We listen to St. John's account of the death of Jesus. Prayers are said for the Church and for those who do not believe in Jesus. We venerate the Cross to show how much we love Jesus. Then we receive Holy Communion.

In all Christian countries, Good Friday is a public holiday. Christians all over the world make a special effort to go to church at 3.00 pm for the Liturgy of the Passion and Death of Jesus.

Pause to discuss

- Why do you think Good Friday is called 'Good'?
- What is the most important action that Jesus did for us on this day?
- In return for what Jesus did for us, what should we try to do for him?

Easter Vigil

The Easter Vigil on Holy Saturday night starts with the service of **'light'**: Jesus Christ is the **Light** of the World.

The church is in total darkness to represent a world without Jesus. The Liturgy begins outside the church with the lighting of the **Paschal Candle** from the new **fire**. The people light their candles from the Paschal Candle and then bring the light into the church.

After the priest has carried the candle into the dark church, he solemnly proclaims that Jesus is risen; this is done through the singing of the

'E X U L T E T'.

This is one of the most ancient prayers of the Church.

There are readings which recall the history of God's love and promises. Then, we hear the Gospel account of the Resurrection of Jesus from the dead. After this, people who want to become Catholics are baptised and receive the Sacrament of Confirmation. Everyone renews their baptismal promises and Mass is celebrated in a very joyful way.

Activities

1. Make a chart to show the most important links between what happened in the Gospels and what happens in Church during Holy Week.

Mk 11:1-10	Passion Sunday …
Jn 13:3-5; 1 Cor 11:23-26	Holy Thursday evening …
Matt 26:47-56	Holy Thursday night …
Matt 27:45-54	Good Friday …
Matt 28:1-8	Easter Sunday …

2. Choose one of the Holy Week Liturgies.
   Show how it is based on the Gospel accounts of the life of Jesus.
   For example: what happened in the Gospel and how this event is re-lived in the liturgy.

3. Design a reminder about 'Holy Week Services in Church' for your school notice board, website or newsletter.
   a) Briefly explain what will happen.
   b) Give reasons why it is important to participate in these services.
     (If possible, find out if there are special Liturgies for children in the Parish).

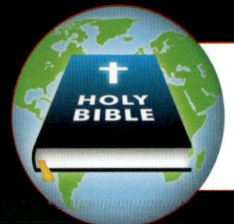

**Know about the Ascension.
Reflect on what it was like for the disciples.**

Disciples of Jesus

When God chooses people, he does not always choose the good, the great and the best, he chooses ordinary people like us.

When Jesus chose the first disciples, he knew their weaknesses but he also knew that by his power and grace he could transform them.

At first, life for the twelve disciples was an exciting adventure. They felt privileged to be chosen, as everyone was amazed at their Master's teaching, the parables he told and the miracles he worked.

The disciples were with Jesus when violent waves were breaking right over their boat. They witnessed him rebuke the winds and the sea, and all was calm again (Matt 8:23-27).

They saw men strip away the roof over a place where Jesus was and lower a paralysed man down into the room. To their amazement, Jesus not only cured the man, but also forgave his sins (Mk 2:1-12).

Yet they did not fully understand who he was, that he was truly God as well as truly human. Jesus did not lose faith, hope and trust in them. In fact, he was about to make them missionaries for the world! What does this tell you about Jesus?

Mission to the world

After his resurrection, Jesus appeared to the disciples many times, but on this last occasion they were to become Apostles. Jesus said, "**All authority in heaven and on earth has been given to me. Go, therefore, make disciples of all the nations; baptise them in the name of the Father and of the Son and of the Holy Spirit.**

Teach them to observe all the commands I gave you. And know that I am with you always; yes, to the end of time" (Matt 28:16-20).

The Ascension

The Apostles were greatly puzzled. Jesus told them that they would receive power when the Holy Spirit came on them. Then they would be his witnesses, not only in Jerusalem, but throughout Judea and Samaria, and even to the ends of the earth.

Jesus was lifted up while they looked on, and a cloud took him from their sight. They were still staring into the sky when suddenly two men in white were standing near them and they said, "Why are you men from Galilee standing here looking into the sky? Jesus who has been taken up from you into heaven, this same Jesus will come back in the same way as you have seen him go there" (Acts 1:11).

The Apostles returned to Jerusalem. They were joined by Mary, the mother of Jesus, together with several women. They locked themselves in the upper room and prayed continuously (cf. Acts 1:12-14).

Pause to discuss

- What evidence is there that Jesus still trusted his Apostles?
- What does that tell you about him?
- What do you think the Apostles said to one another when they saw Jesus vanish from their sight?
- Why do you think they locked themselves into the Upper Room?

1. Imagine you are one of the Apostles. You have to prepare to go out to the whole world to baptise and teach the people about Jesus.

a) First you must reflect on the advice Jesus gave you:

| Jn 14:27 | Jn 15:7 | Jn 15:20 | Jn 16:33 |

b) Give reasons for:
- what you like about this mission;
- what you would find difficult;
- what you would fear most of all;
- what would keep you going when life was challenging.

2. Plan your Mission. Think about the teaching of Jesus and his advice.

a) Where would you like to go? Why?
b) Make a list of the main points of your teaching.
c) What would you take with you?
d) What must you remember to do? Why?

3. a) How can you be a young apostle today?
   b) What could you do?
   c) What might you want to share with others?
   d) How would others know you were fully committed to living out your Faith?

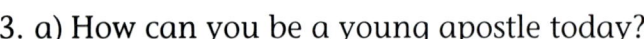

Pentecost

**Understand what happened at Pentecost.
Reflect on how the Spirit transformed the Apostles.**

Power of the Holy Spirit

The Apostles were huddled together in fear of their lives.

"Suddenly they heard what sounded like a powerful wind from heaven, the noise of which filled the entire house in which they were sitting; and something appeared to them that seemed like tongues of fire; these separated and came to rest on the head of each of them. They were all filled with the Holy Spirit, and began to speak foreign languages as the Spirit gave them all the gift of speech" (Acts 2:1-4).

Through God's Spirit, the Apostles were changed so that:

- cowardice gave way to courage;
- unbelief became a flame of faith;
- doubt changed to conviction that nothing on earth could shake;
- fear was banished and the Apostles were afraid of no one, no threat, no danger.

Ready for Mission

Now these fear-filled Apostles felt **brave, courageous, strong** and ready for anything! "Everyone was amazed and unable to explain it; they asked one another what it all meant. Some, however, laughed it off. 'They have been drinking too much new wine,' they said" (Acts 2:12-13).

Then Peter leaped up the steps of a nearby building. He began to speak, loudly with authority and conviction, to thousands of people:

"Men of Judea, and all you who live in Jerusalem, make no mistake about this, but listen carefully to what I say. These men are not drunk, as you imagine; why, it is only the third hour of the day."

Peter reminded the people that God had sent Jesus to them and they knew him by the signs and miracles that he worked. Yet they allowed him to be crucified. Jesus was killed but God raised him to life. Jesus, who is now with the Father, has sent the Holy Spirit.

The First Conversions

Hearing what Peter was saying, "the people were cut to the heart and said to Peter and the Apostles, *"What must we do, brothers?"*

"You must repent", Peter answered, *"and every one of you must be baptised in the name of Jesus Christ for the forgiveness of your sins, and you will receive the gift of the Holy Spirit. The promise that was made is for you and your children; and for all those who are far away, for all those whom the Lord our God will call to Himself."*

Peter spoke to them for a long time using many arguments, and he urged them, *"Save yourselves from this crooked generation".*

They were convinced by his arguments, and they accepted what he said and were baptised. That very day about three thousand were added to their number." (Acts 2: 14-41 abridged)

DISCIPLES ABANDON LEADER
They legged it, say guards

THE ROCK'S SHATTERING DENIALS
Servant woman speaks out

DISCIPLES REFUSE TO BELIEVE 'RISEN AGAIN' RUMOURS
Women told to stop dreaming

FOLLOWERS OF NAZARENE DAZZLE PENTECOST CROWDS
Everyone understood, says witness

DRUNK ON WINE AT NINE?
Sect leaders are drunkards, say some

3000 JOIN NEW SECT AFTER PREACHING OF GALILEANS
Crucified leader has risen, say followers

1. Study these sensational headlines relating to the disciples 'BEFORE' and 'AFTER' they received the Holy Spirit.
   Choose one '**before**' and one '**after**' and provide the evidence for it. (Clues for 'before' see Matthew 26 and for 'after' see Acts 2).

2. **Witness to the Truth.**
   Write an article for the '**Jerusalem Daily**'.
   Mention:
   a) what actually happened at Pentecost,
   b) a summary of what Peter said,
   c) why so many wanted to be baptised,
   d) the message we must not ignore!

Peter the Apostle

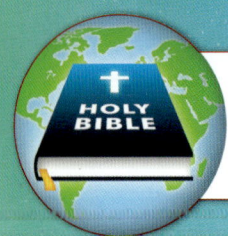

Deepen our understanding of Peter, the Apostle. Reflect on how the Holy Spirit transformed him.

Power of the Spirit

Not long after winning over three thousand new converts, "Peter and John were going up to the Temple for the prayers at the ninth hour. It happened that there was a man being carried past. He was a cripple from birth; and they used to put him down every day near the Temple entrance called the Beautiful Gate so that he could beg from the people going in" (Acts 3:1-2).

Activity

a) Read about the cure of the man who could not walk (Acts 3:1-10).

b) Write a script for the six pictures above.

c) Why do you think Peter was able to work this miracle?

d) Mention three effects the miracle had on the man.

Peter cures a paralytic at Lydda

"Peter visited one place after another and eventually came to the saints living down at Lydda. There he found a man called Aeneas, a paralytic who had been bedridden for eight years. Peter said to him 'Aeneas, Jesus Christ cures you: get up and fold up your sleeping mat'. Aeneas got up immediately; everybody who lived in Lydda and Sharon saw him, and they were all converted to the Lord" (Acts 9:32-35).

Peter raises a woman to life

At Jaffa there was a woman disciple called Tabitha. She was always doing good and helping others. The time came when she became ill and died. They washed her and laid her out in a room upstairs. The disciples sent for Peter to come as soon as possible.

As soon as he arrived, Peter was taken up to the room. He asked everyone to leave. He knelt down and prayed. Then he turned to the dead woman and said, "'Tabitha, stand up'. She opened her eyes, looked at Peter and sat up. Peter helped her to her feet. Then he called the saints and widows and showed them that she was alive. The whole of Jaffa heard about it and many believed in the Lord" (Acts 9: 40-42).

Activities

1. Even though Jesus was no longer with Peter, he was **IN** him.
   Identify the evidence.

2. Read '**A miraculous escape**' (Acts 12:1-19).
   a) What do you think Jesus wanted Peter to learn from his experience in prison?
   b) How do you think Peter's story might have helped his friends?
   c) Give examples of how it might help you or other people today.

Early Christian Community

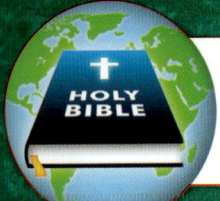

Understand how the Holy Spirit worked through the Apostles.
Reflect on how the experience of the Apostles can help us.

The Early Christians

It was around this time that the early Christian community was formed. "The whole group of believers was united, heart and soul; no one claimed for his own use anything that he had, as everything they owned was held in common. They continued to witness to the resurrection of the Lord Jesus with great power, and they were all given great respect" (Acts 4:32-33).

The power of the Holy Spirit

"So many signs and wonders were worked among the people at the hands of the Apostles that the sick were even taken out into the streets. They were laid on beds and sleeping-mats in the hope that at least the shadow of Peter might fall across some of them as he went past. People even came crowding in from the towns round about Jerusalem, bringing with them their sick and those tormented by unclean spirits, and all of them were cured" (Acts 5:12-16).

Pause to discuss

- In what ways did the Apostles change?
- What attracted the people to them?
- Give examples of how the Holy Spirit worked in and through them.

Activities

1. Investigate the account of the Apostles' arrest and their miraculous escape.

   Here are the facts. Find the evidence in Acts 5:17-42 and write the reference for each one.

   a) Jealousy prompted the high priest and his supporters to arrest the Apostles.

   b) At night the angel of the Lord opened the prison gates and led the Apostles out.

   c) Next morning, the officials found the jail securely locked, the guard on duty, but when the door was unlocked there were no prisoners inside.

   d) Peter and the Apostles reminded the High Priest and his council that they had executed Jesus and that God had raised him up.

   e) Gamaliel, a Pharisee, warned the high priest and council to leave these men alone. He said that if their enterprise was of human origin it would break up, but if it was from God, they would not be able to destroy it.

   f) Evidence that the Apostles were flogged and felt it was an honour.

2. Imagine the following question is put to you by the high priest and his council. "Tell us, what exactly turned a group of cowards who used to meet in secret into a group of fearless preachers?"
   Give your opinion and support your answer with evidence.

3. a) Give examples of situations where Christians have been persecuted. (PPP Persecution of Christians DVD ROM 6)

   b) In what ways is the Holy Spirit likely to help Christians who are being persecuted for their faith?

4. Watch the YouTube 'Myriam's Story & Song' (DVD ROM 6).
   Many people believe Myriam is a 'shining star'.
   Give reasons why you think people are able to say this about her.
   What message would you like to send to her?

Paul the Apostle

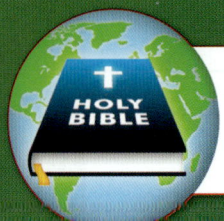

Understand the transformation that took place in Paul. Reflect on how Paul's teaching can help us.

Saul of Tarsus

Saul was a Pharisee, a Jew who followed the Jewish religious law strictly and made sure everyone observed it. As the Christians were not following the law, he believed it was his duty to persecute them and put them in prison.

Saul encounters Jesus

Saul was out to slaughter the Lord's disciples. "Suddenly, while he was travelling to Damascus and just before he reached the city, there came a light from heaven all round him. He fell to the ground, and then he heard a voice saying, **'Saul, Saul, why are you persecuting me?'** 'Who are you, Lord?' he asked, and the voice answered, **'I am Jesus, and you are persecuting me. Get up now and go into the city, and you will be told what you have to do.'**

The men travelling with Saul stood there speechless, for though they heard the voice they could see no one. Saul got up from the ground, but even with his eyes wide open he could see nothing at all, and they had to lead him into Damascus by the hand. For three days, he was without his sight and took neither food nor drink" (Acts 9:3-9).

Pause to discuss

- In what way was Saul persecuting Jesus?
- What is the very important lesson we must learn from what Jesus said to him? Give examples to explain it.

Saul becomes Paul the Apostle

Ananias, who lived in Damascus, had a vision in which the Lord told him to go to Saul. Surprised by this request, Ananias asked the Lord if he knew about all the harm Saul had been doing to the Christians. The Lord replied, "You must go all the same, because this man is my chosen instrument" (Acts 9:15).

Ananias went to Saul. "He entered the house, and at once laid his hands on Saul and said, 'Brother Saul, I have been sent by the Lord Jesus who appeared to you on your way here so that you may recover your sight and be filled with the Holy Spirit'.

Immediately it was as though scales fell away from Saul's eyes and he could see again. He was baptised there and then" (Acts 9:17-19). From that time onwards, Saul's life was turned upside down! As a result of this transformation, Saul became known as Paul.

Pause to discuss

- What do you think Jesus meant when he said to Ananias, 'This man is my chosen instrument'?
- What kind of challenges do you think Paul may have to face next?

(See also questions in TB pp.68-69)

Paul's mission

Paul visited Cyprus, Turkey, Rome and many other places. At different times, he travelled with Barnabas, Silas, Timothy and Luke. Together they had many adventures.

Paul writes,

- Five times I have been given the thirty-nine lashes;
- three times I have been beaten with sticks;
- once I was stoned;
- three times I have been shipwrecked, and
- I have been in the open sea for a night and a day.

"I have been in danger from rivers, in danger from brigands, in danger from my own people and in danger from the Gentiles (non-Jews), in danger in the towns and in danger in the open country, in danger at sea and in danger from people masquerading as brothers. I have worked with unsparing energy, for many nights without sleep, I have been hungry and thirsty and often altogether without food or drink; I have been cold and lacking clothing" (2 Cor 11:24-27).

Paul's character

Once Paul understood who Jesus was, he dedicated his life completely to him. It did not matter what it cost him, he wanted to serve Jesus for the rest of his life. Nothing would stop him: exhaustion, suffering, poverty or danger of death. In fact, he welcomed them because they helped him to become more like his Master, Jesus. He never forgot how he had persecuted the early Christians. All the great things he succeeded in doing helped to deepen his faith in Jesus. He attributed all his success to the Spirit of Jesus working in and through him.

Paul's last journey

Paul's missionary journeys had included Syria, Turkey, Cyprus and Greece where he performed numerous miracles. When Paul returned to Jerusalem, he

was involved in serious conflict with some Jews. He was arrested and imprisoned for two years. It was decided that Paul should be sent to Rome where he was to stand trial for his alleged crimes.

Paul was handed over with other prisoners to a centurion called Julius. On the way to Rome, gale force winds battered the ship. The sailors even threw the ship's equipment overboard to try to lighten the load. Paul advised them, "I ask you not to give way to despair. There will be no loss of life at all, only the ship". Paul was about to show to Julius, the crew and the prisoners that God was with them. (cf. Acts 27)

Activities

1. a) What were the hardships and sufferings that Paul experienced?
   b) Why and how did he manage to persevere?

2. Work in groups. Imagine you are the prisoners and are now in Malta.
   Prepare to be interviewed by the local TV news channel.
   a) Each group takes one of the references from the Acts of the Apostles:

   | 27: 23-26 | 27:30-38 | 27: 41-44 | 28: 1-6 | 28: 7-10 |

   b) In preparation, read and summarize the text.
   c) Give a dramatic report of the events on the **Evening News**.

3. **Shipwreck: God's ways are mysterious!**
   Judge, select and decide on the various means God used to bring Christianity to Malta. Make a thinking map to illustrate your views.

Paul reflects on his experience

When Paul looked back on his mission, he could see that wherever he had gone to teach the people about Jesus, there had been suffering and persecution. Yet, always, there were people who believed and were baptised. He understood that when his suffering was greatest, he opened his heart to God pleading for help. Gradually, he understood that God worked best, God's power was greatest, when he totally relied on Him.

What does Paul teach us?

We must learn to trust in God and put ourselves totally in His hands. God does always answer our prayer, but like a loving parent, God knows that what we ask for is not always good for us. So, sometimes He says, 'No'!

Paul wants us to understand that he experienced many hardships: he was whipped, shipwrecked and even beaten up. Nevertheless, he was so convinced that Jesus was in him and **working through him** that he could say, **"I live now not my own life, but with the life of Jesus who lives in me"** (Gal 2:20).

Paul shows us that Jesus is alive now. Jesus speaks to us now and is always ready to help us.

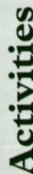

Activities

1. Hot-seating: Paul. Prepare the questions. (WS DVD ROM 6).

2. a) What were the two most important lessons that Paul had to learn?
   b) Give examples of how these lessons could help you.

3. "St. Paul is the greatest of all the Apostles." Discuss.
   (Guidance in TB p.71 & DVD ROM 6)

4. Think of how Paul's experience might help a refugee, a family break up or someone with a serious illness. Choose one and give examples.

Successors of St. Peter

Peter, the first Pope

During his lifetime, Jesus made Peter the leader of the Church to take over when he went back to heaven. Jesus said to Peter,

"I say that you are Peter (the rock) and on this rock I will build my Church.... I will give you the keys of the Kingdom of heaven" (Matt 16:18-19).

Jesus is the head of the Church but he gave Peter the authority to act in his name, to teach what is true and condemn what is false in matters of faith and morals.

"Anyone who listens to you listens to me; anyone who rejects you rejects me and those who reject me reject the one who sent me" (Lk 10:16).

Down through the ages, this authority has been passed on from pope to pope in the Catholic Church.

Successors of St. Peter

The Pope represents Jesus in a special way. With the bishops, he guides the Church in matters of faith and morals.

There have been more than two hundred popes since the time of St. Peter. Let us look at some of the most recent ones.

St. John Paul II (1978-2005)

Pope John Paul II was a true missionary. He could speak ten languages, a gift which helped him when he visited over one hundred and forty countries. He was like a loving father to all the people. Everywhere he went, thousands and thousands flocked to hear him speak about Jesus. Young people loved him. Almost every year, he called them together for a 'World Youth Day' to share experiences of living their faith, to pray, to celebrate Mass and to have fun. Pope John Paul was canonized in 2014.

Pope Benedict XVI (2005-2013)

Pope Benedict wanted young people to be saints not celebrities. He said, "What God wants most of all for each one of you, is that you should become holy. He loves you much more than you could ever begin to imagine, and He wants the best for you. I know that the best thing for you is to grow in holiness".

Pope Benedict XVI was very humble. In 2013 because of his age and frailty, he could no longer do the work required of a pope, so he retired.

Pope Francis

Pope Francis was elected on 13 March 2013. He is noted for his humility, care, compassion and mercy. What he says and does frequently makes headline news, **"Rock star Pope takes the world by storm"**. He implores the crowds to think of the prospect of meeting one's maker as something to look forward to, like a wedding, where Jesus and all of the saints in heaven will be waiting with open arms.

Pope Francis speaks to young people

"I asked you the question: Where is your treasure? In what does your heart find its rest? Our hearts can be attached to true or false treasures: they can find genuine rest or they can simply slumber and become lazy. The greatest good we can have in life is our relationship with God. Are you convinced of this? Do you realize how much you are worth in the eyes of God? Do you know that you are loved and welcomed by him unconditionally, as indeed you are?"

"I ask you all … but **reply in the silence of your heart**, not aloud:
Do I pray? **Do I speak with Jesus**, or am I frightened of silence? Do I allow the Holy Spirit to speak in my heart? Do I ask Jesus: What do you want me to do, what do you want from my life?
Speak continually to Jesus in good times and in the bad."

"Jesus offers us something bigger than the World Cup! Something better than the World Cup! **Jesus offers us** the possibility of a fruitful life, a life of happiness; he also offers us **a future with him**, an endless future, in eternal life. That is what Jesus offers us. But he asks us to pay admission, and the cost of admission is that we train ourselves 'to get in shape,' so that we can face every situation in life undaunted, bearing witness to our faith."

Address, World Youth Day, July 27, 2013

Activities

1. Take time to reflect carefully on what Pope Francis says to all young people.
   a) What does he say Jesus offers us?
   b) What is the admission price?
   c) What guidance does Pope Francis offer us to help us face every situation in life and witness to our faith?
   d) What would you find most challenging in the advice he gives?

2. Research the life of one of the Popes.
   Give reasons why you think millions of people all over the world find meaning and purpose in his teaching and example.

6. Called to Serve

Understand that we are all called to be disciples.
Reflect on our response to this invitation.

The Invitation

For most of us, our invitation to be a disciple arrives when we are baptised. This is when we enter into the life of Jesus and receive his Spirit. We become members of the Church and Jesus helps us to live a good life.

In the Sacrament of Baptism, we are each invited to be a disciple. It is a bit like receiving an invitation card with the instructions about what we must do in order to take part. With this invitation to be a disciple, comes the gifts we need in order to accept it. As we grow older and prepare for the Sacrament of Confirmation, we must consider the invitation for ourselves and what it is that Jesus is asking of us.

YOU can Change the World
Jesus invites YOU to be a disciple.
He wants you to build up the Kingdom of God.
Use all your gifts to spread the Good News.
By serving others, you will be serving Jesus.
RSVP

Pause to reflect

There is no one on this earth like you. Who you are and what you have is unique. Only you can take the part that is meant for you. Stay close to Jesus; he will show you what is really and truly important in life.

Reflection

"God has created me to do Him some service;
He has committed some work to me
which He has not committed to another.
I have my mission …
I am a link in a chain, a bond of connection
between persons.
I shall do good, I shall do His work.
Therefore, I will trust Him.
Whatever, wherever I am, I cannot be thrown away."

Blessed John Henry Newman, extract from *Some Definite Service*

As Christians, we believe we have a mission in life. Our mission is a special way in which we can use our gifts and offer them back to God.

Activities

1. Design an acrostic with the word 'UNIQUE'. Try to get across:
   - that there is no one like you,
   - that you have a special mission in life.

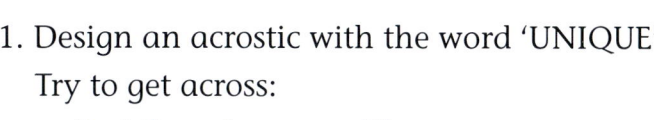

U nlike any other
N ew path for me
I n the depths of my h...
Q
U
E

2. a) Read and reflect on the **invitation**.
   b) Write a reply to Jesus. In it, be sure to focus on each line of the invitation. Mention your beliefs and values.

3. Some of the things Jesus said to the disciples are listed in the box. They are from Mark's Gospel.

   a) Choose any three sayings. After reading them, try to explain how the first disciples might have put these words into action.

   b) Try to explain how you might put these words into action today.

Follow me (1:17)

Come away to some lonely place (6:31)

Forget self (8:34)

Take up your cross (8:34)

Be a servant (10:44)

Be on your guard (13:33)

Stay with me (14:32)

Go out to the whole world and proclaim the Gospel (16:15)

Sacrament of Confirmation

Understand what the Sacrament of Confirmation does for us.
Reflect on how we could use the gifts of the Holy Spirit.

The Sacrament of Confirmation

The Sacrament of Confirmation gives us the gifts of the Holy Spirit. We are given these gifts not to keep for ourselves, but to use to help others. We are called by God to live more like Jesus and to share in the work of Jesus in our world.

Gift of the Holy Spirit

When a person is being confirmed the Bishop prays for the **gift of the Holy Spirit** for those who are about to receive the Sacrament.

When the Bishop prays over the candidates and anoints them with holy oil, God's blessing descends on them. It brings a special strength to spread and defend the faith by word and action as true witnesses of Jesus.

Anointing with Chrism symbolises the strength the candidate is given to share in the work of spreading the Kingdom of God.

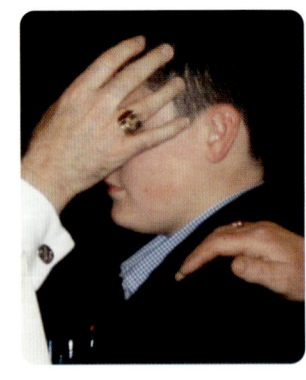

By this anointing, the person receives the 'mark', that is the *seal* of the **Holy Spirit**. This seal marks our total belonging to **Jesus** and our enrolment in his service forever.

Pause to discuss

What responsibilities come with this Sacrament? Give examples.

Gifts of the Holy Spirit

In the Sacrament of Confirmation, God gives us the gifts of the Holy Spirit.

If we truly understand these gifts and believe that we receive them in this Sacrament, then it is possible for our lives to be transformed.

The gifts of the Holy Spirit help us to be true witnesses to our faith and build up the Kingdom of God wherever we are in the world.

Wisdom

Understanding

Right Judgement

Courage

Knowledge

Reverence

Awe and Wonder

Wisdom
To have wisdom is to see things as God sees them. It helps us to follow the way of God by making right decisions.

Understanding
This is the gift that helps us to understand all that Jesus has told us.

Knowledge
This gift will help us to recognise the goodness and greatness of God and to see the world as it really is.

Courage
To have courage is to do the right thing even when you are afraid. Physical courage is risking your own safety for what is right. Moral courage is risking your relationship with others for what is right.

Right Judgement
This gift will help us to know what is right and what is wrong when faced with difficult situations.

Reverence
This gift helps us to love God and each other. It urges us to give glory to God in everything we do.

Wonder and Awe
The gift of wonder and awe helps us to appreciate that:
God is infinite and infinitely mysterious;
this infinite God loves each one of us;
God's creation is beautiful and inspiring.

1. Choose two gifts of the Holy Spirit.
   Give examples to explain what they mean.
   Share with the class.

2. Think of the difficulties some young people experience.
   What gifts do you think they need most of all to help them?
   Give reasons.

3. a) Make a list of the main reasons for receiving the
      Sacrament of Confirmation.
   b) Draft a letter to your Parish Priest to explain why you
      would like to receive the Sacrament of Confirmation.

4. "The world of today needs fully committed
   young Christians".
   a) Why do you think the world needs
      fully committed young Christians?
   b) In what ways can you witness to
      your faith?
      Think of the challenges you could
      encounter and how you can rise
      above them.

5. **Prepare for a Quiz. Work in teams.**
Below are the answers. Write the questions.

a) The teacher collects the questions, checks them and puts them in a box.

b) Pupils take turns to pick a question to ask the rest of the class.

(i) Confirmation is one of the seven Sacraments of the Church.

(ii) Sacraments are the way God has chosen to give us a share in his own divine life.

(iii) Confirmation strengthens and perfects the grace given to you at Baptism.

(iv) You must want to receive the Sacrament of Confirmation; that is, it must be your decision.

(v) You need to be in the state of grace; that means you will not have chosen to deliberately turn away from God and from the Church.

(vi) You need to know and understand what Jesus and the Church teach us about what to believe and how to live a good life.

(vii) You will need to receive the Sacrament of Penance before Confirmation so that you are fully prepared.

(viii) You need a sponsor to pray for you and to help you.

(ix) It gives us a special strength of the Holy Spirit to spread and defend the faith by work and action as true witnesses of Jesus Christ.

(x) Like Baptism it can only be received once, for it puts a spiritual mark on our soul which can never be removed.

Sacrament of Marriage

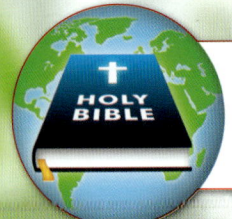

Know about the Sacrament of Marriage.
Reflect on the importance of this Sacrament.

A Covenant

The Sacrament of Marriage is a **covenant**, that is, a solemn promise between a husband and wife. It is based on faith, hope and love.

- **Faith** in God.

- **Hope** in God's help to remain faithful to the promises made.

- **Love** of God and one another.

It is a solemn promise to be faithful to each other forever: in good times and in bad times, in sickness and in health, for better or for worse.

The Sacrament of Marriage

In and through the Sacrament of Marriage, God dwells with the husband and wife. He is with them in their happiness and He gives them the grace to forgive each other when things go wrong. This grace comes through daily prayer. Every effort to love and help each other brings God's blessings.

The Sacrament of Marriage is a life-long and life-giving commitment. The husband and wife are open to the possibility of having children and promise to bring them up in the Catholic faith. However, there will be lots of challenges and at times, it will be very difficult, but God will always be there to help and support them.

The couple enter the Sacrament of Marriage through the vows they make at their wedding ceremony. If this takes place at a Mass, the vows come after the reading of the Gospel and the homily. The Mass is called a Nuptial Mass.

The ceremony begins when the priest welcomes the couple, their family and friends. He assures them that Jesus blesses their love abundantly.

Statement of Intention

The priest asks the bride and bridegroom if they:

- have come freely and without reservation to give themselves to each other in marriage;

- will love each other as husband and wife for the rest of their lives;

- will accept children lovingly from God and bring them up according to the Law of Christ and his Church.

Making Vows

The priest invites the bride and the bridegroom to join their right hands and declare their consent before God and His Church.

In turn they say:

"I . . . . . take you . . . . . to be my lawful wedded wife/husband, to have and to hold from this day forward, for better or for worse, for richer or for poorer, in sickness and in health, to love and to cherish, till death do us part".

Blessing and Exchange of Rings

The priest blesses their rings as a sign of their love and fidelity and prays that they will always have a deep love for each other. The rings are circles which are symbols of eternity. This reminds the couple of God's eternal love for them and of their love for each other.

The husband then places his wife's ring on her finger. Then she does the same for him. At the same time, they say together, "In the name of the Father and of the Son and of the Holy Spirit. Amen".

Nuptial Blessing

This is a special blessing for the married couple.

- Father, keep them always true to your commandments.

- Keep them faithful in marriage and let them be living examples of Christian life.

- Bless them with children and help them be good parents.

- Give them the strength which comes from the Gospel so that they may be witnesses of Jesus to others.

Activities

1. Work in pairs.
   a) Think of the three best reasons for getting married.
   b) Write them in the order of importance.
   c) Share with the class and agree on the three most important.

2. a) What responsibilities do parents have to help to build up the Kingdom of God?
   b) Suggest ways children can help their parents to do this.

3. Explain the meaning and purpose of the Sacrament of Marriage.
   Mention:
   - what the Sacrament is and what it involves,
   - the purpose and importance of the vows, the rings and the blessing.

4. 'Marriage takes Three'. Re-read the text on page 110 and explain what this means.

Sacrament of Holy Orders

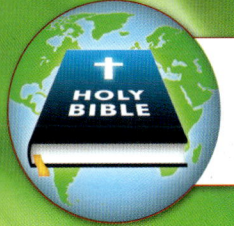

**Know about the Sacrament of Holy Orders.
Reflect on this special way to serve God and others.**

The Threefold Ministry

Holy Orders is the Sacrament through which the mission entrusted by Jesus to his Apostles is to be carried on in the Church until the end of time. It includes three degrees: bishop, priest and deacon. Each one is ordained by the Sacrament of Holy Orders.

Quick Quiz

a) What evidence is there in the Bible that Jesus:
- authorised the first Apostles to teach in his name?
- promised to be with them always, even to the end of time?

b) What were the names of the Twelve Apostles?

Deacons

In the ordination of deacons, the candidates are appointed to a special service within the sacrament of Holy Orders. They represent Jesus as the one who came "not to be served but to serve, and to give his life as a ransom for many" (Matt 20:28). Deacons proclaim the Gospel, preach and teach. As ministers of the Sacraments, they can baptise, witness marriages and conduct funerals.

Priests

The Sacrament of Holy Orders gives a special grace of the Holy Spirit to those who are about to become priests. When a man is ordained a priest, the Holy Spirit shapes and moulds him so that he can represent Jesus. The Holy Spirit gives a special **seal** which is an indelible mark on the soul. When the priest receives this **seal**, he represents Jesus as a shepherd who looks after his flock.

Bishops

Bishops must first of all be apostles, that is, faithful witnesses of Jesus who personally called them to follow him and then sent them out. Their mission is to bring Jesus to all the people and lead all the people to Jesus. This happens through their preaching, the celebrations of the sacraments and their responsibility for a diocese, that is, a cluster of parishes. Together with the Pope they are responsible for the entire Church.

Rite of the Sacrament of Holy Orders

On the day of Ordination for a priest, the ceremony is full of outward signs to show the new life of the priest.

When the candidate lies prostrate on the floor, it symbolizes:
- his unworthiness for the priesthood,
- his dependence upon God,
- his need for the prayers of the Christian community.

Everyone present calls upon the saints to help him.

Laying on of Hands

The Bishop places his hands on the head of the candidate. This is a gesture of calling down the Holy Spirit and the Bishop prays the prayer of Consecration. At this moment, the sacrament takes effect.

Vesting

The new priest receives the stole which is worn around his neck. Then he is given the chasuble. It is the vestment worn at Mass as a symbol of service to God and His people.

Anointing

The Bishop anoints the palms of the priest's hands with the oil of chrism. This is an outward sign of the inner sealing of the priest's heart which is totally dedicated to God.

The new priest receives the bread and wine to be offered in the Mass that he will now celebrate with the Bishop.

Activities

1. What is the ministry of a deacon? Give examples.

2. What does the Sacrament of Holy Orders actually do for a priest?

3. What are the three most important responsibilities of a bishop?

4. What diocese do you live in?
   What is the name of your Bishop?

5. Explain what beliefs and values you think might inspire a young person to become a deacon or a priest.
   Think about:
   • what the Sacrament does for the candidate,
   • what a deacon or priest is able to do for others,
   • the values that are likely to inspire and motivate him.

**Understand that there are many ways to serve.
Reflect on a variety of ways to help others.**

Helping Others

Every day, God comes to us in a variety of ways: for example, in prayer or through other people. We are His disciples and each day He gives us opportunities to show our love by helping others.

Annalena Tonelli (1943-2003)

When Annalena was just five years old, she knew what she wanted to do with her life. She felt the need to serve people who were suffering and rejected, who were crying out for help.

When she was 26, she left Italy for Africa to begin her life's work among the unloved and marginalised. Annalena totally respected everyone she met, no matter how they appeared or what their religion.

Tuberculosis (TB) is a disease which can now be controlled by medicine, but when Annalena went to Kenya, TB killed thousands of people each year. She gained qualifications in treating TB and set up centres which cared for and cured hundreds of people. She also worked with deaf children who had been written off by their families. She educated them. She taught them skills so that they could work and become independent. One young woman said, 'Before Annalena, we were nothing'.

In 1984, the Kenyan government rounded up men and boys from the area where Annalena was working. They were suspected of being bandits and the government planned to kill them. Annalena stood up to the authorities and drove out to the airfield where the men were being held.

She buried those who had already been killed and took survivors back to her hospital for treatment. The publicity which followed this violent event led to Annalena being expelled from Kenya.

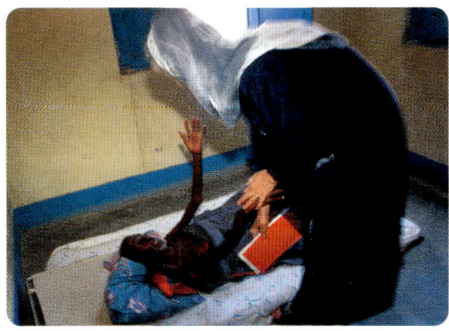

She went to Somalia to continue her work with TB patients and train Somali doctors and nurses. This was the time of a terrible famine in Somalia. Annalena set up a centre to feed and nurse famine victims. Her schools for deaf children were also re-established. Annalena helped elderly people who had lost their sight. She brought doctors from Germany to perform a simple cataract operation to restore their vision. The elderly people had given up hope. However, when they could see 'they became human beings again'. Annalena had restored their dignity.

Annalena was a devout Catholic living and working in a Muslim society. She knew of no other Christians in the area. She lived her life for Jesus, 'crying out the Gospel with her life'. She is an example of someone who lived her whole life serving others as Jesus asked. She worked in Africa for over thirty years dedicating her life to the destitute and needy.

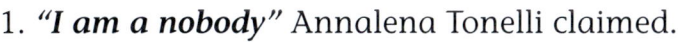

Annalena's life of care and compassion ended violently in 2003. She was shot as she left her hospital. Her killer has never been found.

Activities

1. **"I am a nobody"** Annalena Tonelli claimed.
   a) Reflect on her life and mission.
   b) Do you agree with her self-assessment? Why or why not?
   c) Give a different opinion and say why some people might hold it.
   d) Say why you disagree with this opinion.

2. Annalena lived a life of radical poverty, yet she saw her life as pure joy rather than sacrifice.
   a) What evidence is there in Annalena's life which shows that she lived a life of poverty.
   b) Why do you think she experienced pure joy rather than sacrifice?

Sr. Joan O'Callaghan CP (1931-1982)

When Sr. Joan saw the extreme poverty of the people in Villa El Salvador, a desert area near Lima in Peru, she felt called to this mission.

In this shanty town, seventy percent of the people were unemployed. At least eighty per cent of the children suffered from malnutrition. Sr. Joan became involved immediately. She helped a group of women to set up a 'Mission Breakfast and Dinner' scheme. They fed ten thousand children who would otherwise have lived on the verge of starvation.

Sister Joan spent many years feeding the hungry and teaching the people about the life of Jesus. She gave the people a great love for the Bible and they continue to tell others how the 'Word of God' changed their lives.

On 31 December 1982, Sr. Joan was very badly injured in a car crash and died two weeks later. She was buried amongst the poorest in Villa El Salvador – this was her wish.

Activities

1. Read the account of Sr. Joan's mission (DVD ROM 6).
   a) In what ways do you think her work was inspired by the gifts of the Holy Spirit?
   b) Name the gifts you think she used most of all and explain how she used them.

2. Read about the mission of sixteen year old Pauline Jaricot, (TB page 86 and DVD ROM 6).
   If Pauline was alive today, what do you think she would consider as the greatest spiritual needs in our country?
   a) Try to give specific examples.
   b) Why do you think these needs exist?

Responses to God's Call

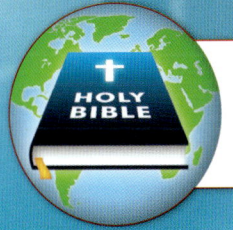

Turn, Drop, Trust

When Jesus called his disciples, what did he ask them to do? Let us think about three things:

'Turn' their vision and aim towards his mission.

'Drop' everything that would hinder them from fulfilling this mission.

'Trust' by doing their very best and always trusting in God's help.

God's Call

God works in mysterious ways in the life of each one of us. For Maggie Gobran, God's call initially appeared totally crazy to those close to her.

Mama Maggie

Mama Maggie is the name given to Maggie Gobran by children in the slums of Cairo in Egypt. She is married to Ibraham Abouseif, who is a successful business man, compassionate and kind. They have a son and a daughter. Maggie first worked as a marketing executive and then as a professor of computer science at Cairo's American University.

One Christmas, Maggie visited a rubbish dump to give presents to the poor. She noticed something moving around and when she looked closely, she found a small child buried in the rubbish, then another. She could not believe human beings could survive like this. She saw

children competing with rats for bits of discarded bread. They had nothing: no clean water, no electricity, no schools, nobody to care for them.

On another occasion, she said, "I found a widow who couldn't find a pair of shoes for her daughter. When I took her little girl to get shoes she said: 'I want a bigger size.' I asked the girl why. 'For my mother, she doesn't have any shoes,' the girl replied. I thought: "What a spirit of sacrifice that she thought of her mother rather than herself". On other visits, Maggie washed the children's feet which were covered with sores and dirt.

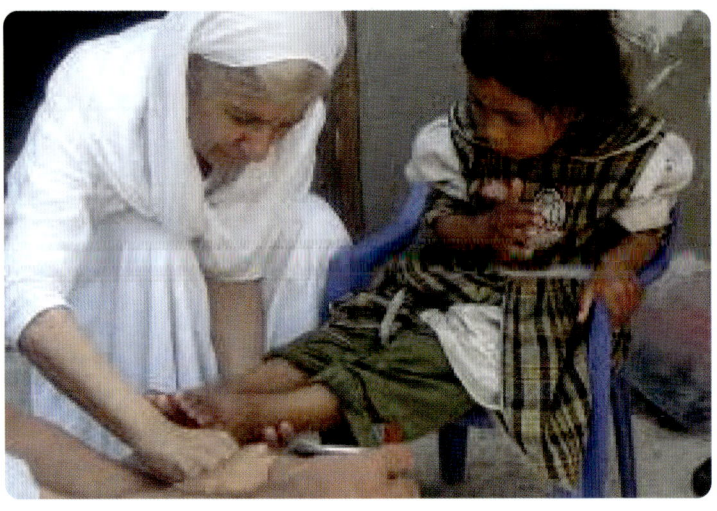

In 1998, Maggie spent three days in prayer. She recalls saying to God, "You are a merciful God. How can you allow this tough life for innocent children?" A clear voice inside her seemed to reply, "It is up to you to do something". On reflection, she thought, "These children are my chance to be a better person". She knew she had to do something more to help.

On another visit to this garbage site, Maggie took a business man with her. When he saw the situation, he advised her that it was a hopeless case. The people were living in shacks without proper ceilings. When it rained, the water just poured into the rooms. The needs of these people were overwhelming. However, Maggie believed not in her own strength, but in God who could work through her. If it was God's will for her to help the people on this garbage site, she could rely totally on Him.

Maggie gave up her work at the university, sold her jewellery and some of her personal possessions. With the help of her husband and family, she set up a charity, 'Stephen's Children'; named after St. Stephen who was stoned to death

for being a Christian and became the first martyr. She wanted to help these destitute children to know that they are all loved by Jesus. Every day, in schools, established by Maggie, the children say, **"I can do all things in Jesus because he strengthens me"**.

Mission of Stephen's Children

The mission is to help save lives, bring hope, and restore dignity to under-privileged children and young people. Mama Maggie and her teams work in the slum areas of Egypt, seeking to build strong trusting relationships with the poorest, most vulnerable children and their families. The aim is to nurture, train, and equip  underprivileged children and young people, morally, educationally and spiritually.

As Christian missionaries, the main purpose of the teams is to bring the children who are nominal Christians to the knowledge and love of Jesus and the Church. This mission began about twenty-five years ago and still continues today.

Pause to discuss

- What means did God use to call Maggie Gobran to a new mission?
- Was she right to give up a good teaching post at the university to do this work? Give reasons for your answer.
- What would you have done in her situation?

Activities

1. Reflect on the life of Mama Maggie.
   Using '**Turn**', '**Drop**', '**Trust**', explain how she responded to God's call.

2. "**These children are my chance to be a better person.**"
   - Explain what you think Mama Maggie means by this.
   - Do you agree with her? Why or why not?
   - Give a different point of view and say why some people may hold it.
   - Say why you disagree with it.
   - What do you think Jesus would say?

Be a Living Witness

**Understand what it means to be a disciple now.
Reflect on ways to use your gifts now and in the future.**

You are unique

You are very special.

In all the world there is nobody like you.

Since the beginning of the world there has never been another person like you.

Nobody has your smile, your eyes, your hands, your hair.

Nobody owns your handwriting, your voice; you're special.

Nobody can be a disciple just like you – Jesus needs you.

What Makes You Unique?

Activity

To be a disciple means to live out the New Commandment each day.
Watch the Power Point presentation to help you reflect on the many ways to help. Write down the ways you can help others this week.

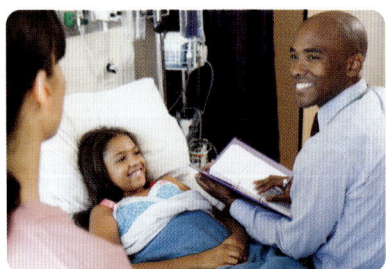

the power of sharing

DONATE!

Thinking Back – Looking Forward

You are now almost at the end of this academic year and may be moving to another school in the autumn. You will be meeting new pupils and making many new friends. You may come to know many young people of other religions. You are likely to be asked about your beliefs and how your faith influences the way you live.

Think of all that you have been studying this year in Religious Education:

The Kingdom of God	Jesus the Messiah
Justice	The Transforming Spirit
Exploring the Mass	Called to Serve

1. a) Which section of the Religious Education programme have you enjoyed most of all? Give reasons.
   b) What are the most important points you have learnt about your faith?
   c) Give examples of how you are able to put your beliefs into practice.

2. Explain how your Religious Education lessons this year have helped to give meaning and purpose to your life.

3. Project:
   Work in groups. The teacher will give you a module to work on.
   Part 1 - Write down all the questions you want to ask on it.
   Part 2 - Write down the answers to the questions.
   Part 3 - The teacher will check the questions and answers.
   Part 4 - Another group will be in the 'Hot Seats' and you will put your questions to them.

Glossary

Annunciation when the angel Gabriel brought God's message to Mary that He wanted her to be the mother of His son, Jesus

Apostle 'one sent out' to preach the Good News

Apostles' Creed a prayer which summarizes our Christian beliefs

Ascension when Jesus went back to heaven, forty days after his resurrection from the dead

Blessed Sacrament the real presence of Jesus in the form of consecrated bread

Bishop a priest who is chosen to be leader of a diocese; he is a successor of the Apostles

Canonize when the Church declares a dead person to be a saint

Carmelite nun a woman who has given her life totally to Jesus. She desires to follow him through a life dedicated to prayer

Cathedral the main church in a diocese

Christ another word for Messiah; both mean 'Anointed One' in English

Civil rights the right to be free from unfair treatment or discrimination, for example, in education, employment, housing, etc

Commissioned to be entrusted with a task

Covenant a very serious promise between God and people, or between two people

Disciple 'learner or follower'; the disciples followed Jesus during his ministry on earth in order to learn from him

Easter Sunday the day when Jesus rose from the dead

Eternal life the life with God in heaven which Christians hope to have forever after they die

Eternity	the endless period of life after death
Frankincense	a spice burned to make a sweet smell, a gift for a king
Fruits of the Spirit	gifts from God
Grace	a helpful gift which comes from God
Genuflect	to go down on the right knee, in the presence of the Blessed Sacrament when you enter or leave the church
Hades	the underworld
Handmaid	a female servant
High priest	the senior Jewish leader
Holy Spirit	third person of the Blessed Trinity
Hosanna	a greeting and an expression of praise and reverence
Incarnation	when the Son of God became man
Indelible mark	a mark that cannot be removed
Last Supper	the meal associated with the Passover, which Jesus celebrated with his disciples in the Upper Room the night before he died
Levite	a priest of the tribe of Levi
Liturgy	worshiping God in public prayer – for example ceremonies in church
Keys of the Kingdom of heaven	the phrase means the power to rule the Church: Here Kingdom of heaven does not mean heaven but the Church – the Kingdom as instituted by Jesus here on earth.
Kingdom of God	reign of God

Magnificat	the song of praise Mary sang to God at Elizabeth's house (Lk 1:46-55)
Magi	wise men from the East skilled in the study of the stars
Messiah	also known as the Christ; the leader longed for by the people of Israel; a Hebrew word meaning 'anointed one by God' and consecrated to Him
Monstrance	a vessel in which the Blessed Sacrament is shown for adoration
Myrrh	a spice used to put on the bodies of people who have died
Nazareth	a town in Galilee where Jesus was brought up
Paschal Candle	Easter Candle
Passover meal	the special meal that Jews have to remember their escape from Egypt
Pentecost	an important Jewish feast day and the day when the Holy Spirit came down on the Apostles
Pharisee	a member of a strict sect of people who observed all the Jewish laws and customs
Pope	a word meaning 'father'; the person who takes the place of St. Peter as leader of the Church on earth
Prodigal	wasteful and extravagant
Sacrament	a very important gift from Jesus, when we receive special help and grace
Sadducees	were wealthy and held positions of power including chief priest and high priest. They were members of the Sanhedrin, the ruling council
Salvation	being saved, being completely close to God
Samaritans	people who lived in the Northern Kingdom of Israel, in Samaria

Sanhedrin	Jewish Council
Saviour	the One who is to save us from sin
Scribes	those who made and kept copies of the Law and helped to interpret the Law
Scripture	another word for the writings in the Bible
Son of David	the one from the lineage of David
Son of Man	Jesus is the Messiah and he is also truly a human being
Soul	the invisible part of you which makes you human and will live forever
Spirit	the part of a person's mind which is able to think
Spiritual	of the spirit rather than the body
Synagogue	a place of worship and learning for Jewish people
Tabernacle	a special, secure container in which the Blessed Sacrament is reserved. It is usually found in a prominent place in the church
Upper Room	the place where Jesus met with his Apostles
Visitation	the time when Mary went to see her cousin Elizabeth
Vocation	a way of life to which a person is called by God
Wise men	also known as the 'Magi' or 'Kings', they made a very long journey to visit the baby Jesus

Acknowledgments

Second and new edition: June 2016

Nihil obstat: Father Terry Tastard

Imprimatur: His Eminence Cardinal Vincent Nichols, Archbishop of Westminster, 15 March 2016.

The *Nihil obstat* and *Imprimatur* are a declaration that the books and contents of the CD ROM are free from doctrinal or moral error. It is not implied that those who have granted the *Nihil obstat* and the *Imprimatur* agree with the contents, opinions or statements expressed.

Theological Advisor: Fr. Bryan Lobo SJ, Pontifical Gregorian University, Rome
Picture Research: Sr. Marcellina Cooney CP

© 2016 Sr Marcellina Cooney CP – Design & Text
© 2016 Ian Curtis, First Sight Graphics, firstsightgraphics.com – Design, Compilation & Format

Illustrations: © Jenny Williams, © Philip Hood, © Peter Dennis

Acknowledgements
Considerable thanks are due to the head teachers of the following schools for making it possible for their teachers to attend Editorial Meetings: Rosary Catholic Primary, Camden NW3 2AE; St. Bernadette's Catholic Primary, London Colney AL2 1NL; St. Christina's Independent, St. John's Wood, NW8 7PY; St. George's Junior, Weybridge KT13; St. Margaret Clitherow Catholic Primary, Stevenage SG2 8RH; St. Simon of England Catholic Primary, Kent TN23.

Permission credits
Cover stained glass window & page 89 © jorisvo/Shutterstock.com; page 4 © jpegwiz, Jayakumar, Value Vitaly, Hung Chung Chih, lanych/Shutterstock.com; page 5 © Yulia Glam, Freer, Alexmillos, Morozov Andrew, Lurin, Zurigeta, Neff, Waddell Images, Ford Contributor, Andi Berger/Shutterstock.com; page 6 © Timmary, sss 615, La lavande/Shutterstock.com; page 7 © Anton_Ivanov, Alexander Raths, Jayakumar, Value Vitaly/Shutterstock.com; page 8 © jprgwiz, Kowition, Rawpixel.com, Thomas Knoch, Ocskay Bence, Luis Louro/Shutterstock.com; page 9 © Fedor Salivanov/Shutterstock.com; page 10 © sibgat,Zvonimir Atletic, bellena/Shutterstock.com; page 11 © jpegwiz, Hung Chung Chih/Shutterstock.com; page 12 © iQoncept, S_oleg, Olga Maslov/Shutterstock.com; page 13 © dizain, Foot Too, Andi Berger, Barabasa, Ilakov Filimonov/Shutterstock.com; page 14 © Kostasgr, Valua Vitaly/Shutterstock.com; page 15 © iQoncept/Shutterstock.com; page 16 © iQoncept, Nataliia Popova/Shutterstock.com; page 17 © Serhiy Kobyakov, Suzanne Tucker, Reservoir Dots/Shutterstock.com; page 19 © Nata-Lia, Syda productions/Shutterstock.com; page 20 © Rawpixel.com, Sarahdesign/Shutterstock.com; page 24 © jpegwiz, Nihongo, MG-S, Path Doc/Shutterstock.com; page 25 © Jiri Miklo, Monkey Business Images, Nataliia Popova, Path Doc/Shutterstock.com; page 26 Corgarashu, Thomas Pavelka, Giambra/Shutterstock.com; page 27 © Laremenko Sergii, jannoon028, Thomas Koch/Shutterstock.com; page 29 © Sunsinger/Shutterstock.com; page 30 © Ricardo Reithmeyer/Shutterstock.com; page 31 © Raw pixel, Photo Stock Image/Shutterstock.com; page 32 © Monkey Business Images, Alexmillos/shutterstock.com; page 34 & 35 © Pierre-Yves Bableon/Shutterstock.com; page 35 © Aptyp-kok/Bigstockphoto.com; page 36 © Lieven VK; pages 38, 39, 42 & 43 © ITV Global Entertainment; page 41 © Notkoo, Murphy 81, 1000 Words/shutterstock.com; page 43 © sibgat, Losw, Rogue Design/Shutterstock.com; page 44 © Miro Kovacevic, Wavebreakermedia, Anelina/Shutterstock.com; page 47 © Zvonimir Atletic/Shutterstock.com; page 49, 50, 55, 57 & 58 © Radiant Light.com, Blend images, Serzh/Shutterstock.com; page 51 © Maxi_m/Shutterstock.com; page 52 © mariusz szczygiel/Shutterstock.com; page 54 & 59 © Catalin Petolea, Zvonimir Atletic/Shutterstock.com; page 58 iQoncept/Shutterstock.com; page 60 © stained glass window from St Aloysius Catholic Church, London NW1 with permission of Rev James McNicholas PP, Aleksander Sadkov/Shutterstock.com; page 64 © Africa Studio, Sirikorn thamniyom, S-F, Syda productions, Chris from Paris/Shutterstock.com; page 65 Vg studio, Pressmaster/Shutterstock.com; page 66 © Sarawut Padungkwan, Vg Studio/Shutterstock.com; page 67 © Renata Sedmakova/Shutterstock.com; page 68 © Virma V, Ricardo Reitmeyer/Shutterstock.com; page 69, 72, 73, 74,75, 76,77, 78, 80 © ITV Global Entertainment; page 69 © Olga Maslov/Shutterstock.com; page 70 © Ryan Roderick Beiler/Shutterstock.com; page 72 Dmitry design/Shutterstock.com; page 73 © Zvonimir Atletic/Shutterstock.com; page 80 © Vectors 1/Shutterstock.com; page 81 © Amoonrae/Shutterstock.com; pages 82, 83, 84 © Marcellina Cooney CP; page 85 © Mazur/Catholicnews.org.uk, Malu Studio, Yitwang, Nito/Shutterstock.com; Page 86 © Zvonimir Atletic/Shutterstock.com; page 87 & 89 © Jorisvo/Shutterstock.com; page 88 © Arcady, iQoncept, Gustavo Frazao/Shutterstock.com; page 91© iQoncept/Shutterstock.com, Tohn Takai/Bigstock.com; page 93 © Renata Sedmakova/Shutterstock.com; page 95 © Donskarpo, Sara Padunkwan/Shutterstock.com, photo © SAT7; page 97 © Ministero dell'Interno, Italy; pages 98 & 99 © Basilica Papale Di San paolo Fuori Le Mura, Italy; page 100 © Renata Sedmakova/Shutterstock.com; page 101 © AKG Images, Nataliivector/Shutterstock.com; page 102 © Miqu77/Shutterstock.com; page 103 © Izabela Anna, Janonkas/Shutterstock.com; page 104 © Tropinira Olga/Shutterstock.com; page 109 © Denis Cristo, Thomas Reichart/Shutterstock.com; page 108 © Northseapics/Shutterstock.com; page 110 © Jpegwiz/Shutterstock.com; page 111 © graja/Shutterstock.com; pages 114 © Mazur/Catholic news.org.uk; pages 114& 115 © Society of Jesus, UK; pages 119, 120 & 121© Matjaz Kacicnik, Stephen's Children Charity, Nataliia Popova/Shutterstock.com; page 122 © Jacek Dudzinski, Monkey Business Images, Tang Yan Song, Dirk Koebernik, Wavebreakmedia, Speed Kingz, WCKIW/Shutterstock.com; page 123 © Vector Graphics, Crowther.Lindeque/Shutterstock.com

Every effort has been made to contact copyright holders. Any omissions will be rectified in subsequent printing if notice is given to the Teachers' Enterprise in Religious Education Co. Ltd, 40 Duncan Terrace, London N1 8AL

Published by Teachers' Enterprise in Religious Education Co. Ltd, 40 Duncan Terrace, London N1 8AL
www.tere.org

Printed in the UK by Geerings Print Ltd, www.geeringsprint.co.uk